JUMP THE CURVE

50 ESSENTIAL STRATEGIES TO HELP YOUR COMPANY STAY AHEAD OF EMERGING TECHNOLOGIES

Jack Uldrich

PLATINUM PRESS®

Avon, Massachusetts

The Platinum Press® is a registered trademark of F+W Publications, Inc.

Published by
Adams Media, an F+W Publications Company
57 Littlefield Street, Avon, MA 02322. U.S.A.
www.adamsmedia.com

ISBN-13: 978-1-59869-420-8
ISBN-10: 1-59869-420-0

Printed in the United States of America.

J I H G F E D C B A

Library of Congress Cataloging-in-Publication Data
is available from the publisher.

This publication is designed to provide accurate and authoritative information with regard to the subject matter covered. It is sold with the understanding that the publisher is not engaged in rendering legal, accounting, or other professional advice. If legal advice or other expert assistance is required, the services of a competent professional person should be sought.
—From a *Declaration of Principles* jointly adopted by a Committee of the American Bar Association and a Committee of Publishers and Associations

Many of the designations used by manufacturers and sellers to distinguish their product are claimed as trademarks. Where those designations appear in this book and Adams Media was aware of a trademark claim, the designations have been printed with initial capital letters.

This book is available at quantity discounts for bulk purchases.
For information, please call 1-800-289-0963.

To my children, Meghan and Sean . . .

May you always keep your childlike curiosity and believe in doing the impossible.

Contents

Preface and Acknowledgments

This book began rattling around in my head in May 2002 after I had finished reading an interview in *Technology Review*. In it, Nathan Myrhvold—Microsoft's former chief software architect—elucidated upon his theory that the technological revolutions of the twenty-first century would be based on those areas that exponential growth rates take hold. As luck would have it, the very next day I had the opportunity to hear Ray Kurzweil speak at the first ever NanoBusiness Alliance annual meeting in New York City. He had not yet written his book, *The Singularity is Near*, but in his talk Kurzweil painted a compelling picture of how exponential advances across myriad technological fields were conspiring to usher in an era of profound change. The confluence of these two events convinced me that in order to prosper in the early part of the twenty-first century, people of all stripes needed to come to terms with the awesome power of exponential change at some basic level and, more importantly, that they needed tangible methods of dealing with profound change.

Since that time I have spent a great deal of time reading and speaking with a variety of people who have helped shape and inform my particular view of the world, beginning with Messrs

Myrhvold and Kurzweil. I would also like to extend a sincere thanks to every author and writer listed in the bibliography section of this book for taking the time to research, write, and convey the many ideas and examples that either supported my supposition or presented me with a different way of seeing or thinking about the world around me.

In no particular order, I must also acknowledge a special thanks to those individuals who graciously took time out of their busy schedule to speak with me about my ideas and proceeded to take my understanding to a deeper level, including Rodney Brooks, director of the MIT Computer Science and Artificial Intelligence Laboratory; Stu Wolfe, a former official with the Defense Advanced Research Projects Agency and now a professor of material science and physics at the University of Virginia; Steve Jurvetson, a principal partner at the venture capital firm of Draper Fisher Jurvetson; and Josh Wolfe, cofounder and managing partner at Lux Capital and the editor of the *Forbes Wolfe Nanotech Report*. I am indebted to their keen insights. The opinions expressed in the book are mine alone, as are any errors of fact.

Introduction

Never underestimate an exponential.

—Carl Sagan

For reasons I can't entirely recall now, my freshman year of high school began on Friday, September 1, 1978—the day before the Labor Day weekend, which is traditionally regarded as the last official weekend of summer. I will never forget the very first lesson of my first class—Social Studies I. It began promptly at 8:05 A.M. and was taught by Louie Senta. He was a gruff old man with a shock of silver hair and a gravelly voice. If I didn't know better I would have thought he was delivered straight from central casting to play the role of an intimidating disciplinarian—a role, I might add, that he played with a persuasive amount of gusto.

After the bell rang signaling the start of class, Senta rested his steely blue eyes upon his new wide-eyed charges for what seemed like an eternity. He then posed this peculiar question: "If you had a choice between taking $100,000 a day for this entire month or accepting a single penny today and having the penny double every day for the remainder of the month, which would you select?

The class was silent, but I remember thinking, "What a stupid question." Unbowed by the sea of incredulous, pimple-spotted faces staring back at him, Senta asked, "How many of you would choose $100,000 a day?" His face showed no emotion as he paused a moment to let us to ponder our answer.

At the time my only concern was whether the month of September had thirty or thirty-one days and, therefore, whether I would be entitled to the princely sum of $3 million or $3.1 million.

Senta called for a showing of hands. Without bothering to look around the room to seek the assurance of my peers, I shot my hand up. Only afterward did I glance around the room and note with mild satisfaction that my new classmates were just as bright as me.

To confirm what was already obvious, Senta then asked if anyone would choose the second option. No one raised their hand. Then, in a refrain that was to become all too familiar for the next four years of our lives, he ordered us, "Do the math. See how much richer you are because of your wisdom."

Being good with numbers, I quickly doubled the penny ten times and calculated the sum to be $5.12. I continued on for another ten doublings. The figure after the twentieth iteration, I noted with a serene sense of satisfaction, was a scanty $5,242.88. Again, I pressed on in confidence. It was only after the twenty-eighth step—when the figure reached $1,342,177.28—that a sinking feeling came over me and I realized the error of my ways. After the thirtieth and final doubling I calculated I would have been entitled to $5,368,709.12—or almost $2.4 million *more* than if I had taken the "obvious" choice.

In retrospect I suspect that the purpose of Mr. Senta's little exercise was twofold. For starters, the quiz was doubtlessly his way of humbling a bunch of cocky fourteen-year-old know-it-alls and demonstrating to us, in no uncertain terms, that we still had much to learn.

In a larger sense, though, I believe he was trying to teach us a more profound philosophical lesson: Things that might at first appear to be obvious are not always so. While he didn't say it at the time, the implicit message was that it was important to understand the underlying forces that are at work in any given situation.

I tell this little story because, just as my classmates and I didn't appreciate the power of exponential growth with regard to the penny, so many people these days also underestimate the power of exponential growth in other fields. Today there are no fewer than nine technological forces that have been and are continuing to grow at near exponential rates, and unless people begin to come to terms with the momentous changes that are afoot they are going to make some costly mistakes—mistakes that will make my hypothetical loss of $2.4 million look like child's play. The nine technological trends undergoing exponential advancement are computers/semiconductors, data storage, Internet bandwidth, the sequencing of the human genome, brain scanning, artificial intelligence, nanotechnology, robotics, and the advancement of knowledge itself.

Jump the Curve is not, however, a book about technology— although it will document and explore how many of these technological trends will impact the world of commerce. Rather it is a book about change and it will lay out the case for why leaders must welcome change. More importantly, it will provide a number of tangible steps that will help people and organizations embrace radical change in order to tap into the amazing possibilities that these new and profound transformations will create.

Throughout the course of this book the reader will find that I rely on a number of stories and analogies to illustrate many of the points that I am seeking to make. The reason for this is because the majority of people—especially nontechnical people for whom this book is primarily intended—do a better job of absorbing and comprehending stories and analogies than they do complex and arcane lectures about technological trends.

To this end, one of my favorite stories about the power of exponential growth is a story about the pond and the water lily. It can help anyone who needs to be jolted out of his current—or what I called a linear—mode of thinking.

In a nutshell, here's the story: Imagine a small pond that sprouts a single lily on June 1. The lily splits into equal-sized lilies every day for a month. Further assume that the lilies of are such a size that at the end of the month the entire pond is covered with the pesky aquatic plants.

Under such a scenario what percentage of the pond do you imagine would be covered on June 20—or two-thirds of the way into this exercise? One percent? Five percent? Ten percent? Perhaps higher?

I am sorry to say that not only are all of the above guesses wrong, they are, in the words of my old teacher, Mr. Senta, "dangerously wrong." By day twenty lilies cover roughly one one-thousandth of the pond—a wee one-tenth of 1 percent.

What transpires in the next ten days, though, is nothing short of transformational. Here's the math (some of the numbers have been rounded slightly):

Day 20:	.01%	Day 26:	6.25%
Day 21:	.02%	Day 27:	12.5%
Day 22:	.04%	Day 28:	25%
Day 23:	.078%	Day 29:	50%
Day 24:	1.56%	Day 30:	100%
Day 25:	3.125%		

I recount this story because it reveals a common misunderstanding about exponential trends. In the beginning, most people don't even recognize the trend as exponential. For instance, a single lily growing to cover one-tenth of 1 percent of a pond hardly seems noteworthy, let alone deserving of special attention.

The problem with this negligence is that it can cause people to ignore or dismiss some very big and significant trends. All the while exponential math continues to weave its inextricable magic. Unfortunately, all too often, by the time people finally grasp how fast things are progressing—say on day twenty-eight of the pond example—and hope to either capitalize on its explosive growth or, alternatively, avoid being overwhelmed by its growing power, it is too late.

Here's the point: The forces that I mentioned earlier—computers, data storage, Internet bandwidth, the sequencing of the human genome, brain scanning, artificial intelligence, genetic algorithms, robotics, nanotechnology, and knowledge—have been and are all continuing to advance at astounding rates. Yet today they cover only one-tenth of 1 percent of the proverbial pond.

It is essential, therefore, that the forward-thinking executive, whom I've chosen to call the *exponential executive*, think of today as being the metaphorical equivalent of day twenty in the pond analogy. The really big developments are still a few years off in the future, but they are coming fast and the time to begin preparing yourself and your organization for this is *now*. To survive you will need to learn how to jump the curve.

Technology has always been important, but we are standing on the precipice of an inflection point in human history. Technology is reaching what I call the knee of the curve, a point in time in which its exponential growth is taking off at a nearly vertical slope . . . the pace of progress is itself accelerating.

—Ray Kurzweil, *The Singularity Is Near*

CHAPTER 1

Welcome to the Exponential Economy: Prepare to Jump the Curve

Someone once asked Albert Einstein what he considered mankind's most powerful discovery. Without hesitation he replied, "Compound interest." The world's numerati have long been fascinated by the awesome power of geometrical growth, and to prosper in the economy of the future, or what I call the exponential economy, today's leaders must go beyond simple fascination and embrace the extraordinary possibilities that exponential growth portends.

The distinction between linear growth and exponential growth is not merely a matter of degrees. It can literally be the difference between life and death, as the following story demonstrates.

According to legend, the emperor of China, after being presented with the game of chess, was so impressed with it that he offered the inventor—a seemingly humble man—a gift of his choosing. The inventor made a request that on the face of it seemed innocent enough. He requested that he be granted a single grain of rice on the first square of the chessboard, two on the second, four on the third, and so on until all the board's squares were accounted for. The emperor glanced at the board, noted it had only sixty-four squares, and readily granted the man his request.

The story abruptly ends with the emperor severing the inventor's head after only the thirty-second square. This is because, although only halfway through the deal, the emperor was already committed to providing the inventor the equivalent of forty acres worth of rice. Had he lived up to the terms of the agreement, the emperor would have been put in the untenable position of having to supply *18 million trillion* grains of rice. To appreciate this predicament it helps to understand that it would take an area approximately twice the size of the earth, including all of the oceans, to produce that much rice.

YOU AIN'T SEEN NOTHING YET!

Like most fables, the story holds a powerful and valuable lesson and it is one that is especially relevant today: If you think change is happening fast today, you haven't seen anything yet. Consider just the first of many such real-world equivalents of exponential growth: computer transistors. For the past forty years the number of transistors that could be placed on a computer chip has doubled every eighteen to twenty-four months. This development is widely known as Moore's law and is named in honor of Gordon Moore, the former CEO of Intel, who in 1965 accurately predicted this progression.

For years so-called experts have been predicting the imminent demise of Moore's law. Undeterred by such prophecies, talented engineers and technology geeks have ignored their warnings, and in 2007 Intel Corporation and others achieved the twenty-ninth iteration of this doubling. In so doing they successfully squeezed more than 500 million transistors onto a single chip. This astonishing achievement has dropped the cost of one megahertz of computer processing power from $7,000 in 1970 to just fractions of a penny today.

According to the semiconductor industry, there is still clear sailing for Moore's law for at least the next ten years. This means, among other things, that by 2018 computers will become a minimum of thirty-two times more powerful than those existing today.

Using the earlier analogy of the chessboard, with regard to the modern transistor era of computers we have not even approached the halfway point in the doubling game. To put it another way, this means that society is but a *fraction* of the way into the computer revolution. The really big changes are still before us.

The time to begin contemplating what computers thirty-two times more powerful will mean for your business is *now*. To do this you will need to learn to "jump the curve."

To understand what I mean by this term, return for a moment to the example that I cited in the book's introduction of a penny doubling every day for a single month. The graph looks like this:

Exponential Growth

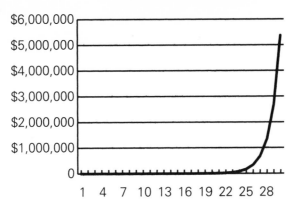

Up until day twenty-three it is difficult to notice any discernible movement. By day twenty-five you can begin to observe a slight inclination up the Y axis, but it hardly looks noteworthy because it appears linear in nature. Only between day twenty-six and day twenty-seven can you notice an inflection point. This is sometimes called the "knee of the curve," and it represents a brief interlude between the more modest, linear-looking aspect of the curve and the much more radical part of the curve that shoots up in an almost vertical fashion.

Exponential INSIGHT

In the game of football, to be an excellent passing quarterback it is not essential to know anything about the physical forces of speed or gravity that affect the ball's movement as it makes its way to the receiver. Rather a good quarterback simply has to anticipate where the receiver will be at a certain time and throw the ball—not to where he is but to where he will be. The same principle is at work for the exponential executive. It is not essential to understand the underlying sciences of biotechnology, nanotechnology, and so forth in order to survive in tomorrow's exponential economy. One must, though, grasp where these trends are headed because that will help gauge the distance one must jump the curve in order to effectively position his or her organization to prosper in the future.

To understand the true implications of the trend, it is necessary to jump the curve and look at how different things are from day twenty-seven—$671,088—to day thirty, when the total has reached $5.368 million. If the chart continued for just another five days, the total would leap to almost $172 million.

The challenge is that it is not just pennies or computer transistors that are growing exponentially, it is data storage, bandwidth, genomics, brain scanning, artificial intelligence, robotics, nanotechnology, and knowledge. Only by jumping the curve can the exponential executive appreciate just how different the future will be from today.

Small opportunities are often the beginning of great enterprises.

—Demosthenes

In periods of profound change, the most dangerous thing is to incrementalize yourself into the future.

—Kurt Yeager

CHAPTER 2

The Power of Zenzizenzizenzic

Knowledge, it has been said, is the key to success. It is a statement that is hard to disagree with unless you buy into that old adage that ignorance is bliss. Proceeding on the assumption that if you believed the latter you probably wouldn't be reading this book, I will go farther out on a limb and state that for years one of the world's better recognized fonts of knowledge has been the *Encyclopedia Britannica*—a reservoir of 30,000-plus pages of information replete with titillating tidbits of data about everything from atoms to zettabytes (a term I will introduce to you later).

In the late 1990s the revered encyclopedia came under assault from a new form of media distribution—the CD-ROM. Able to store vast amounts of information in a more convenient, colorful, and vivid fashion, *Encyclopedia Britannica* was forced to deal with this new competitive threat and proceeded in good haste to provide its information in a similarly fresh, snappy, and visually pleasing format.

By 2001 the company was back on its feet and headed down the sweet path of profitability. No sooner, though, had that storm passed when another began forming on the horizon. But just as a hurricane begins with a single molecule and is not immediately discernible, so was this one.

The storm was called Wikipedia, and it started in 2001 with nothing more than 100 encyclopedia-like entries drafted by a few amateurs and posted to a Web site. It seemed innocent enough. After all, how likely was it that a bunch of strangers, working for free, could someday produce an encyclopedia that would rival the esteemed *Encyclopedia Britannica* in terms of depth, breadth, and accuracy. It sounded about as plausible as a few molecules in the middle of the Atlantic Ocean turning into a Category 5 hurricane.

Yet in late 2005 Wikipedia smashed into the *Encyclopedia Britannica*. That year the prestigious scientific journal *Nature* announced after a comprehensive study that the average entry in Wikipedia was nearly as accurate as the typical *Encyclopedia Britannica* entry.

The advantage is still in *Encyclopedia Britannica*'s favor, but how much longer will it be able to withstand the gale force winds? The answer: not much. That is because we are now living in a world of exponential advances, and the scales are tipped in Wikipedia's favor.

To begin, the very subject matter of the encyclopedia, which is to say knowledge itself, is growing exponentially. It has been said that human knowledge is doubling roughly every seven years. If true—and given how the other forces that will be outlined later in this chapter are adding to the sum total of knowledge—it leads to the almost ridiculously sounding (but mathematically verifiable) conclusion that by 2050 everything we know today will represent less than 1 percent of the sum total of the world's knowledge.

Even if one disagrees with this statement, it is difficult not to acknowledge that radical advances in medicine, physics, chemistry, and biotechnology are changing both the content and value of the material in encyclopedias and that the old print-and-publish method of storing and displaying such information is, if not obsolete, at least impractical.

Neither a printed encyclopedia nor even a CD-ROM can react to this volume of change. Only Wikipedia, by posting information directly to the Internet, can respond in a timely fashion.

Wikipedia also has the advantage in terms of human horse-power. Advances are happening so fast, in so many different fields, that it is virtually impossible for the staff at *Encyclopedia Britannica* to keep pace. The challenge is not nearly so great for Wikipedia because it doesn't have a staff. Instead it relies on a self-selected universe of experts and enthusiasts to keep track of all of these developments.

Third, Wikipedia has a distinct economic advantage. Not only does it not need to print its material in either book or even CD-ROM format, it doesn't need to pay an army of researchers and writers or underwrite the cost of housing any physical resources or employees.

The final kicker is this: Even if the *Encyclopedia Britannica* decides to put all of its content online for free, most people will still go to Wikipedia because its content consistently shows up near the top of most search engines. (A quick search on Google for the terms "atom" or "zettabyte" bears this fact out.)

What *Encyclopedia Britannica* is facing is a severe reaction to the exponential economy, but it is not alone. In fact, if history is any guide, a number of other companies, institutions, and organizations will soon be facing a comparable amount of change in the not-too-distant future.

BROTHER, CAN YOU SPARE A PARADIGM

According to Thomas Kuhn, the famous American intellectual and author of *The Structure of Scientific Revolutions,* a paradigm is defined as a set of practices that define a scientific discipline during a particular period of time. The *Oxford English Dictionary* defines a paradigm as "a pattern or model." In broader terms, in today's vernacular it is often thought of as a specific way of viewing reality.

Using the example of the *Encyclopedia Britannica,* the company's first paradigm was that knowledge was produced by experts, transcribed into books, and sold to customers. In the 1990s the paradigm shifted slightly. Information was still produced by credentialed experts, but it was distributed more regularly and in a digital format.

Sometime around 2005 the paradigm lurched more violently. Information was posted by amateurs to a Web site on a continuous basis and could be accessed by anybody and downloaded for free—in eight languages (and counting) no less.

The example highlights another extraordinary aspect of the exponential economy: The rate of paradigm changes is itself advancing exponentially. According to Ray Kurzweil, author of *The Singularity Is Near: When Humans Transcend Biology,* paradigm shifts are doubling every ten years. To hammer home this point, Kurzweil provides a wonderfully simple way of thinking about these changes.

For starters, he assumes that a paradigm for a business can be said to have shifted when 25 percent of the population incorporates the new technology. By this measure, it took the telephone, from the time it was invented, thirty-five years to be adopted by one-quarter of society. The radio took thirty-one years, the television twenty-six years, the personal computer sixteen years, the Internet seven years, and Wikipedia just five years.

A slightly different prism through which to view this rate of change can be found in Standard & Poor's rating of equity risks, which ranks companies on an alphabetical scale with A+ denoting the least risky and D signifying the most risky. In 1985, 41 percent of all companies earned an A+. By 2006 this figure plummeted to 13 percent. "The future," as Yogi Berra once said, "ain't what it used to be." It is becoming far more risky.

The tangible evidence that paradigms are shifting ever faster is all around us. Since 2001, 50 million (and growing) mp3 players and iPods have changed the way people listen to music. YouTube and video-sharing sites have caused the major television networks to adjust their business models, and the Internet and blogs have changed the nature of the newspaper business and political campaigns.

Ask yourself this: Three years ago would you have been able to define the terms *blog*, *wiki*, and *Wi-Fi* or have been familiar with the terms *RFID* and *Web 2.0*? However, there is no time to even catch your breath because vlogs, mash-ups, WiMAX, Smart Dust, social networking, grid computing, and Web 3.0 are already looming on the horizon.

Now it is not my contention that exponential advances will change *everything*, but I do agree with Warren Buffet's right-hand man, Charlie Munger, who once said that since it is impossible to know everything it is important to load up on a few key insights. The exponential growth of technology is one of those key insights.

Before going any further, let me also add that I agree with Kenneth Boulding, a brilliant Oxford-educated economist, who once said, "Anyone who believes exponential growth can go forever in a finite world is either a madman or economist."

Exponential growth in almost every field does have limits. But—and this is an important but—society is nowhere near the outer limits of the growth that it will experience in computers, data storage, artificial intelligence, genomics, brain scanning, robotics, nanotechnology, and knowledge.

Still, in an effort to avoid long-term prognostications this book will keep the discussion within the realm of the practical by limiting most extrapolations to no more than eight iterations— or doublings—out. Considering that transistors, bandwidth, and the number of gene sequences are all doubling every eighteen months, the number of Internet nodes and brain-scanning capability is doubling every twelve months, and the number of robots is doubling every nine months, this will limit the scope of the discussion to between six and twelve years out. As luck would have it, Wikipedia has provided the perfect word by which to frame these discussions: zenzizenzizenzic.

JUMP THE CURVE STRATEGY #1:
Learn to Spell Zenzizenzizenzic

It should be no surprise that both Google and Wikipedia, as exemplars of exponential growth themselves, have aided in the research of this book. (In 1998 Google's search engines combed through 25 million Web pages. When this book went to print it was up to more than 25 billion Web pages, a thousandfold improvement, and the number of Wikipedia entries has increased from 100 in 2001 to more than 6 million today.)

To this end, I typed the term "exponential" into Google, and the top entry I received back was from Wikipedia. After clicking on a related link called "list of exponential topics," I stumbled upon a small entry at the bottom of one of the pages. It had the word *zenzizenzizenzic* listed.

Being curious, I decided to explore a little further. To my surprise, it brought up another Wikipedia entry. This one offered a definition of the word. Succinctly, zenzizenzizenzic is defined as the eighth power or exponent of a number. For instance, the zenzizenzizenzic of 2 is 256 or 2^8.

In addition to thinking it's a cool, albeit weird, word, I realized that the concept of zenzizenzizenzic was precisely the parameter that I was hoping to put on this book.

Come with me now as we take a short walk into the future as viewed through the power of zenzizenzizenzic.

COMPUTERS: A TRILLION HERE, A TRILLION THERE AND PRETTY SOON YOU'RE TALKING REAL NUMBERS

In August 2006 Cray Inc. installed a supercomputer at Tennessee's Oak Ridge National Laboratory that was capable of performing 54 trillion calculations per second—a sizeable leap over the previous version, which could tabulate a meager 25 trillion calculations. Before I continue any further, let me put the number 54 trillion—54,000,000,000,000—in some context for you:

- 1 million seconds ago was twelve days ago.
- 1 billion seconds ago was thirty years ago.
- 1 trillion seconds ago was approximately 30,000 years ago.
- 54 trillion seconds would put back us over 1.6 million years!

Suffice it to say, 54 trillion is a big number, and researchers at Oak Ridge are applying the brute strength of this supercomputer to tackle a variety of energy-related problems.

Just a few months afterward, however, the federal government announced that it was awarding IBM and Cray a contract to produce a supercomputer capable of 1 quadrillion calculations—or roughly twenty times more powerful—by 2009. In geek speak, the computer will be capable of 1 petaflop. If you're like me and have trouble distinguishing megaflops, gigaflops, teraflops, and petaflops from flip-flops, 1 petaflop means the computer will be capable of 1,000 trillion calculations per second.

Beyond these mind-numbing numbers, the broader point is that all of this computing power will lead to startling new discoveries in material sciences, energy, and biology.

On a level a little closer to home, if your humble laptop computer, which was expected to have somewhere between 500 and 800 million transistors per chip by the end of 2007, continues to double every eighteen months as the Semiconductor Industry Association expects it will, this implies that through a zenzizenzizenzic-like progression the average processor will have 128 billion transistors by 2020. Even if the numbers only double every twenty-four months that would still mean 32 billion transistors will be toiling away on your behalf in about a decade, and the laptop of the future will almost be as powerful as a supercomputer is today.

Another component of the computer that is going through zenzizenzizenzic-like growth is the number of cores being placed on chips. In 2006 Intel and AMD both created the first dual-core chips. In 2007 the companies also introduced quad-core chips, and by 2008 that number could jump as high as eighty. If the industry continues this pace by 2020 chips could have over 1,000 cores.

At a minimum, this suggests that not only will tomorrow's video games be as indistinguishable from today's games as today's are from their early ancestors, such as Pac-Man, but that soon computers will be so smart they will be able to diagnose even the most obscure disease faster and more accurately than today's best doctors and medical specialists.

Exponential INSIGHT

Computers are now on the verge of being so powerful that many in the industry feel computers are leaving the era of search and are entering the era of discovery—where computers will be smart enough to begin anticipating our needs instead of just reacting to them.

DATA STORAGE: STORE THAT THOUGHT

At a technology summit in 2006, I had the opportunity to share the stage with Patrick Burns, an official from Seagate. He noted that in the process of writing and reading data his company's latest HDD disk can spin up to 15,000 rpm and flies just forty atoms above the recording head. Burns went on to share an illuminating analogy to put this feat in some perspective. If the recording head were the size of a 747 jet, he said, the disk would need to be the size of the earth. Therefore, for the jet to perform its job it would fly less than a centimeter off the ground at 800 times the speed of sound. Moreover, it would need to be capable of counting every blade of grass in an area the size of Ireland, while having an error rate of less than ten blades of grass.

What's even more notable is that the next iteration of the data storage technology will fly at the analogy-equivalent rate of 1,600 times the speed of sound, fly only half a centimeter off the ground, and be capable of counting every blade of grass in a country twice the size of Ireland—with only five errors.

At some point this level of progression will cease. But this time is not on the immediate horizon. In 2007 Seagate, Hitachi, and others began selling hard drives capable of storing 1 terabyte of information. (A terabyte, for those with enquiring minds, is an eco-friendly unit of measurement. To store the equivalent amount of information on paper, it would require us to fell 50,000 trees.) By 2010 the industry expects to construct devices capable of storing 300 terabytes—a 300-fold leap—or about the equivalent of storing one year's worth of data from the Earth Orbiting Satellite system.

Beyond that is the exotic-sounding realm of petabytes and exabytes. We should probably stop here because at five exabytes it has been estimated that a single device could hold all the human words ever spoken. (For those interested, beyond exabytes is the land of zettabytes and the very Star Wars-sounding dominion of yottabytes—which is 1,000,000,000,000,000,000,000,000 bytes.)

Let's dial it back to the land of petabytes for the time being. By 2011, it is entirely plausible that 2-petabyte storage systems will be the norm. Two petabytes of information is enough to store all the information in every U.S. academic research library or, alternatively, 2,000 broadcast-quality movies.

Jumping the curve to zenzizenzizenzic requires rationally thinking about the implications of future-generation recording technology not simply recording all of one's conversations but, quite possibly, being able to record everything a person ever sees. To this end, it might interest you to know that Microsoft has a research project called MyLifeBits, which is striving to digitally record every aspect of a person's life. The company is doing this in the expectation that this will soon be an everyday occurrence.

Exponential INSIGHT

One individual who was able to jump the curve in terms of seeing where the data storage industry was headed was Reed Hastings, a former Peace Corps volunteer. In the mid 1990s he was considering starting a business that would mail videocassettes to customers. Due to the expensive nature of manufacturing, duplicating, and mailing videocassettes, Hastings recognized his business plan wasn't practical. Then in 1996 he saw a sample of DVD technology. In a eureka moment, Hastings recognized that not only was digital technology going to get exponentially better as a result of advances in data storage, but within a few years it would be possible to re-create full-length feature movies on DVDs and then distribute them through U.S. mail for the price of a first-class stamp. In 1999 Hastings founded NetFlix, and today it is a $2 billion company and has forced the entire video/home rental market to change its business model or risk being driven out of business.

INTERNET/BANDWIDTH: 2.D'OH!

Having grown up in the Midwest, I had no occasion to give earthquakes much thought. As a result of this unfamilarity, I assumed for years that an earthquake registering 8.1 on the Richter scale was about 10 percent more severe than one registering 7.1 and 20 percent more violent than a 6.1 earthquake.

Boy, was I wrong. For reasons unknown to me, Richter decided it was more appropriate to classify earthquakes on a logarithmic scale. Imagine my surprise then when I learned that this logarithmic scale implied that an earthquake registering 8.1 was 50 times more powerful than a 7.1 earthquake and 2,500 times more powerful than a 6.1 earthquake.

Needless to say, this is important knowledge to possess if you live in an earthquake-prone area. I provide this brief tutorial in logarithmic functions because it is somewhat analogous to the exponential advances society will be experiencing in the development of the Internet.

In spite of the great Internet bubble of 1999, few people would say that the Internet hasn't changed business, society, and many of our lives in meaningful ways. But as unsettling as this may (or may not) have been, it has so far been the equivalent of a technological tremor—it has gotten people's attention, but most have gone about their daily routines.

The transition to the next stage, or what is sometimes referred to as Web 2.0 or the semantic Web, will be a different as a 7.0 earthquake is from a 6.0 earthquake. The next iteration of the World Wide Web will be about relating relevant information to and from real-world objects, and employing intelligent software agents to help users find, store, and combine information in a more useful fashion. The difference can be explained thusly:

Today we find information via Google. At the next level, information will find us.

A variety of technologies, including broadband, RFID, and networks of smart sensors, are all pushing this vision of "the Internet of things" toward reality. But before discussing these technologies, let us first just focus on the transmission of data.

It may be difficult now to remember your first Web experience. If you're like me, it probably occurred over a dial-up modem that connected at a speed of 28.8 kilobytes per second (Kbs). Sometime in the late 1990s, your place of business may have gotten access to a fractional T1 line capable of 256 Kbs, and faxing became increasingly irrelevant because you could just send documents electronically.

Then, sometime around 2002, you probably installed a broadband or DSL line, and within just the past year or so you likely installed a wireless system at home capable of 1,544 Kbs (1.54 MB).

Of course the progress won't stop there. The Institute of Electrical and Electronics Engineers or the IEEE (the engineering group responsible for establishing standards) wants Wi-Fi to be capable of transmitting at least 100 megabits of information per second, and other companies, such as NTT DoCoMo, are looking at rates in the neighborhood of 2.5 gigabits per second—which is fast enough to deliver a DVD in seconds.

Alas, receiving Tom Cruise's latest film via the Internet will only be the beginning. Doctors will be able to send detailed files and images from a patient's medical record to other doctors halfway around the world at the speed of light, search engines will be able to quickly find audio and video files, and students from around the world will be able to watch (for free, I might add) graduate-level courses in biological modeling because IBM has already demonstrated an optical chipset capable of data transmission rates of 160 gigabits per second.

Exponential INSIGHT

Digital and wireless technology are becoming so powerful that in 2005 passengers on a JetBlue plane were able to watch from the comfort (or in this case the discomfort) of their seats live reports on DirecTV of their own plane, which had been crippled by faulty landing gear, as it prepared to make an emergency crash landing. Fortunately everything turned out okay for the passengers, but even a decade ago such a scenario of watching a live digital recording at 30,000 feet would have seemed almost impossible.

Jack Welch once said that "when the rate of change outside the company is faster than the rate of change inside the company, the end is near." Bandwidth and other Internet technologies are now moving so much faster that if a number of industries don't begin reacting soon they, too, could soon be experiencing the horror of watching their own demise as it happens in real time.

BIOTECHNOLOGY: A BRAVE NEW WORLD

In my household, my children have the unusual habit of celebrating half birthdays—the day on which one is precisely halfway between birthdays. My half birthday is January 17—the birthday of one of my heroes, Benjamin Franklin. It just so happened the three hundredth anniversary of Franklin's birth was celebrated on January 17, 2006—my forty-first-and-a-half birthday.

With more than a passing interest, I noted that Franklin lived to the ripe old age of eighty-four and realized that I myself was now approaching my own halfway point in life. This news at first put me in a rather depressed state of mind. Then I stumbled upon some news that changed my outlook. On the same day that America celebrated the tricentennial of Franklin's birth and I celebrated my own half birthday, the Wellcome Trust Sanger Institute announced that it had archived its one billionth DNA sequence. In a nonchalant manner, the press release went on to note that the institute's database was doubling roughly every ten months.

Because a single genetic sequence is kind of like a page of a book, a DNA database containing 1 billion sequences can be thought of as a large book. Only this is no normal book. It is a book that sheds some light on how genetic information might help deliver better health outcomes for all of society.

The story doesn't end with that book, because the first 1 billion sequences is just the first installment of an exponentially expanding number of books. Assuming DNA sequencing continues to double in length every ten months, if one applies a little zenzizenzizenzic to the equation, the Wellcome Trust Sanger database will have 256 billion DNA sequences around the year 2013. Such information, I figured, will most likely keep my heart ticking long past the age of eighty-four.

Already in 2007 doctors are using a limited number of genetic tests to determine which patients will react most favorably to certain cancer treatments. As more genetic information becomes available and massive databases containing genetic information from hundreds of thousands of people are compiled (as is now being done in Britain), the connections between our genes and our health should lead to great change in how we both diagnose and treat disease.

Exponential INSIGHT

Ben Franklin also understood the power of exponential growth. Near the end of his life, rather than accept the $1,000 salary he was offered as president of Pennsylvania—the precursor to today's governorship—Franklin directed that the money be split equally between the cities of Boston and Philadelphia to provide low-interest loans to help tradesmen receive an education. After 100 years of compound interest and growth, Franklin figured that the fund would swell to $100,000. (His prediction was remarkably close.) He then directed that half the proceeds be used to build schools and libraries and that the other half continue to be used for loans.

In another 100 years, he estimated the total would reach $4 million. He directed that the money then be disbursed for educational projects. In Philadelphia the proceeds were used to built the Franklin Institute, and in Boston the Benjamin Franklin Institute of Technology. Even small sums, when compounded over time, can lead to big change, and such will be the case with biotechnology—only over a much shorter timeframe.

BRAIN SCANNING: A PENNY FOR YOUR THOUGHTS

In November 2006, Paul Allen (the lesser-known cofounder of Microsoft) spent $41 million to create an electronic atlas showing which genes switched on neurons in a mouse's brain. The technology might not sound like much, but a senior official at Genentech, one of the world's leading biotechnology companies, said its significance was "on par with the human genome project."

Consider next that IBM, in partnership with the Ecole Polytechnique Fédérale de Lausanne, is spearheading a joint research initiative known as the Blue Brain Project. The project's stated aim is to take human brain research "to a new level." To do this, the team is applying the massive computational capacity of IBM's Blue Gene supercomputer to create a detailed 3-D model of the circuitry in the neocortex—the biggest and most complex part of the human brain—in hopes of shedding light on internal cognitive processes such as thought, perception, and memory.

Of course, this is just the beginning. Ray Kurzweil has suggested that brain-scanning technology is doubling at a rate of every nine months. What then is possible through the power of zenzizenzizenzic in the next six years as these advances in brain-scanning technology are combined with Paul Allen's genetic research and the Blue Brain Project?

At a minimum, the possibilities for advances in psychiatric disorders such as autism, schizophrenia, and depression become much more plausible. Even such mysterious and intriguing aspects of our lives as consciousness—what it is, how it originated, and how it works—could become candidates for serious research.

Exponential INSIGHT

Ninety-five percent of everything learned about the human brain has been discovered within the past twenty years. As a result of this knowledge, researchers now know more about everything from Alzheimer's to how clever marketing impacts different parts of our brain. But this is just the tip of the iceberg. What people think or, more specifically, what they think they know about their own actions will likely undergo a profound transition in the years ahead as neuroscientists uncover new information about how the human brain really operates and influences our behavior.

ROBOTICS: MEET YOUR NEW NEIGHBORS

In the early morning light of March 13, 2004, a dozen robots set off in the Mojave Desert to claim a $2 million prize for being the first robot to successfully navigate a 132-mile course without any human assistance. Only hours later, every robot had failed in the quest. To add insult to injury, none made it farther than seven miles.

The following year, many of the same teams, as well as some new ones, returned to take another stab at the prize. Amazingly, not only did most of the robots surpass the previous mark of seven miles, but in a stunning bout of progress five robots completed the entire 132-mile trek. The winning robot, constructed by a team of engineering students from Stanford University, navigated the course in about seven hours.

The story demonstrates the extraordinary amount of progress being made in the field of robotics. According to one report, the number of robots being used around the globe is doubling every nine months. In 2007 there are an estimated 2 million personal robots (vacuum cleaners, scrubbers, and so on) employed around the world. By 2009 the International Federation of Robotics estimates there will be 9 million.

In 2005 Intuitive Surgical reported that its da Vinci robots were performing 20 percent of all prostatectomies. By the end of 2006 the figure had increased to 35 percent. It won't stop there. Intuitive Surgical thinks it can capture a larger slice of the prostatectomy market and also begin making inroads in performing general surgeries, hysterectomies, and even certain heart procedures.

On a different front, the U.S. Defense Department is so pleased with the performance of robots in Iraq that by 2015 it expects that one-third of all units engaging in combat will be robots. To bring this vision to reality it is investing a significant portion of the $125 billion Future Combat System budget on robotic technology. And as if this isn't enough, the government of South Korea has publicly stated that it wants a robot in every household by 2020.

On the outer edges of robotic technology, students at Stanford University have already designed a robot that can assemble an Ikea bookshelf, load a dishwasher, and take out the trash, and researchers in South Korea have built a robot named Ever-1 that is a human-looking android and can recognize 400 words.

> ## Exponential **INSIGHT**
>
> In an interesting bit of exponential trivia, if Ever-1's 400-word vocabulary undergoes a zenzizenzizenzic-like progression for the next six years, she should know about 25,000 words. Shakespeare himself was said to have known only 29,000 words. If one further sprinkles a dash of zenzizenzizenzic on robots and then jumps the curve, the idea of robots battling alongside our soldiers, building and constructing homes, and assisting octogenarians with household chores not only sounds plausible, it is quite likely. As Bill Gates wrote in the January 2007 edition of *Scientific American,* we are at the "dawn of the age of the robots."

GENETIC ALGORITHMS: SOFTWARE GETS "GO"ING

Although superpowerful computers have now defeated the world's best chess players, there is one board game where humans still reign supreme over computers. It is called Go, and it is an ancient Chinese game that pits the strategic thinking of two players as each takes turns placing stones on a grid with nineteen intersecting lines. Briefly, the goal is to secure as much territory as possible with one's stones.

The game is vastly more complex than it sounds because the numbers of possible moves is far greater than chess, and a single move can trigger a cascade of other possibilities. The permutations are so vast that even smaller versions of the game (it also comes in a thirteen-line variety) can flummox today's most powerful supercomputers.

Before you breathe a sigh of relief and give thanks that humans have at least one place where we can still beat computers, consider that a separate group of computer specialists are now devising algorithms that can contemplate every move and play a large sample of games to see what unfolds. If the program determines that the computer will win more than 80 percent of the games after a particular move, it considers the move to be a good one.

Another way to think of this is that these programs consider every move then select only the ones that appear to have the best "genes." By constantly selecting the best offspring from every subsequent move, the relentless process—just as in evolution—will yield a superior outcome, or in this case, victory. As it stood in mid 2007, a computer was already the world's 2,323rd ranked Go player. Will the algorithms get better? Of course.

To understand just how good such algorithms are becoming, consider these two examples in conjunction with one another. IVL Technologies now boasts that its On-Key Pro Karaoke system can transform a person's off-key voice and make it sound Barbara Streisand–perfect. (If you don't like Streisand, it can also give your voice an edgier and raspier Bob Dylan-esque sound.) But musical technology is not content with making karaoke better. Scientists at MIT have now developed software algorithms that allow people with no musical knowledge or aptitude to get in touch with their inner Bach and compose music.

The point is that software is now getting so good that people with no innate musical skill or knowledge of composing music will soon be able to easily create, compose, and perform music that meets professional standards. Sound unlikely? Consider this: Ten years ago, how many people would have imagined that a full-length movie could be shot on a cell phone, easily edited on a personal computer, downloaded to YouTube in minutes, and watched by millions of people?

Exponential **INSIGHT**

Where will all of this lead? It is difficult to say. A zenzizen-zizenzic leap down just eight generations of mutations of genetic algorithms is vastly more difficult than, say, describing how you are different from your descendants of eight generations ago. In spite of a common lineage, I doubt many of us would recognize, let alone have much in common, with our great-great-great-great-great-great-great-grandfather or grandmother. The difference, of course, is that most of these genetic algorithms are not mutating once every twenty-five years; they are doing it around the clock, 365 days a year.

NANOTECHNOLOGY: THE NEW ALCHEMISTS

In 1984 the first cell phone was about the size of a brick and cost $4,295. Today people wear cyborglike ear-fitting phones that have Bluetooth connections, which can be voice activated, and be purchased at a local retailer for less than $100. Much of this progress has been driven by the miniaturization of electronics.

Similarly, ten years ago if an automobile manufacturer wanted a custom mold it hired a master craftsman who would then sculpt the piece over the course of a few weeks and charge a pretty penny. Today a number of companies specialize in rapid prototype manufacturing and design 3-D models of car parts and body designs for NASCAR cars on the fly and often in a matter of hours. Much of this progress has been driven by the development of more sophisticated modeling software and custom materials.

What happens when miniaturization, complex 3-D modeling, and new materials are combined at the molecular level? One answer is nanotechnology, which is briefly defined "as the willful manipulation of atoms and molecules."

It is an incredibly complex field, and I have written a couple of books on the topic, but for the purposes of our discussion I will greatly simplify it by concentrating on how nanotechnology will impact the field of material sciences.

One way to think of nanotechnology is to picture a modest lump of coal and an exquisite diamond ring. Once you have done so, I'd like to ask a simple question. What are both products made of?

If you were paying attention in high-school chemistry class you'll recall the answer is carbon atoms. You will also recognize that a lump of coal is not nearly as valuable as, say, a two-carat diamond. The difference in value is determined by the molecular structure of the carbon atoms. Therein lies the immense opportunity of nanotechnology.

By willfully manipulating carbon atoms, two companies—Apollo Diamond and Gemesis Corporation—have figured out how to place carbon atoms exactly where they want and in the process have created two-carat diamonds in a matter of days. (Mother Nature requires million of years to do the same thing.)

This, however, is just the tip of the iceberg. A variety of other materials, in addition to diamonds, can be tweaked, grown, and otherwise imbued with new or enhanced characteristics. To date, nanotechnology has already brought society such mundane consumer items as stainproof khakis, scratch-resistant paints, antifogging mirrors, and self-cleaning glass, but extraordinary advances in plastics, glass, and metals are also possible.

The really big discoveries, though, lie just ahead. Nanotechnology promises to deliver everything from materials that are a hundred times stronger than steel but have one-sixth the density to materials that can self-heal and devices so small they can penetrate individual cancer cells and deliver cancer-killing drug molecules.

Exponential INSIGHT

The exponential executive does not need to understand how nanotechnology works, but he or she does need to be aware of its existence because if Apollo Diamond and Gemesis can double their diamond production from today's level of .003 percent for each of the next eight years, they could be producing 38 percent of the world's diamonds by 2016. What else is possible with nanotechnology when viewed through the prism of zenzizenzizenzic? One possibility beyond the world of material science, according to the National Cancer Institute, is that cancer could become a manageable disease by 2015 as a result of extraordinary progress that is being made in nanotechnology today.

JUMP THE CURVE STRATEGY #2:
Take a Bird's-Eye View of the World of Tomorrow

Without question, one of the most extraordinary exponential thinkers the world has ever known was Leonardo da Vinci. In the early sixteenth century, he was already envisioning helicopter-like contraptions, tanks, bicycles, calculators, and even the concentrated use of solar power.

Lesser known than many of his other works of art is a painting called *The Bird's Eye-View of a Landscape.* In it, da Vinci paints the Tuscan landscape as imagined from the perspective of a bird. The painting is remarkable because the viewpoint is far higher than any building in Florence could have afforded da Vinci at that time.

The painting required da Vinci to envision himself on a perch a few thousand feet high. Interestingly, if da Vinci were six feet in height, through the power of zenzizenzizenzic he would have reached 1,536 feet—or about the perspective from which the landscape was painted. The challenge for the exponential executive is to do the same with tomorrow's business landscape. If you do extrapolate all of the aforementioned technological advances out over the next decade, the view is sure to astound you.

First we build the tools, then they build us.

—Marshall McLuhan

Each stage of evolution provides more powerful tools for the next.

—Ray Kurzweil

CHAPTER 3

Exponential Enablers

If all of the aforementioned advances are enough to make your head swim, I am afraid I have some bad news for you. Things are only going to grow more complex. This is because many of these advances are not confined to their own fields; they are crashing and converging into one another in unexpected and exciting ways.

One simple story captures the essence of this convergence. In the fall of 2006, a woman named Claudia Mitchell, who had lost her right arm in a motorcycle accident in 2004, lifted a cup for an audience of reporters. What made the demonstration so astonishing is that she used nothing but her mind to move and control the prosthetic arm attached to her body.

The display was a testament to the power of convergence. First surgeons rewired a small patch of skin on her chest to act as a sort of biological control panel for her arm and hands. They did this by attaching the stumps of the nerves of the arm (which were still intact after the accident) to other nerves in the chest. This allowed Mitchell to send a "message" down the nerves when she wanted to lift her arm or squeeze her hand.

Once there, small electrodes placed on her chest interpreted the signals and relayed them to a computer inside the robotic arm (which is attached at the chest) where the signals were then translated into the corresponding action that Mitchell was thinking.

The device is only a prototype, but as sensors, computers, robotics, neural implants, and brain-machine interface technology continues to improve, future devices will only get better. In fact, doctors soon hope to give Mitchell's robotic arm and hand the sensation of feeling.

AN AUTOCATALYTIC PROCESS

There is no single reason why all of these advances are occurring now, but a large part of the answer lies in the equipment. Each generation of equipment begets a new generation of even better equipment.

Consider computers again. Today silicon is the main material used in the manufacture of computer chips. Component parts on the circuits are now growing so small and are being packed so close together that the electrons are zipping around so fast that they are threatening to literally melt the silicon.

To solve this problem, the computers themselves are being used to design and model new nanomaterials, which might be able to replace silicon within the next years. In fact, in 2007 IBM and Intel both announced they would be switching to a new hybrid material in 2008.

What is really interesting, though, is that these new chips will be turned around and used in next-generation computers, and those next-generation computers will then help design the next round of new materials. This is called an autocatalytic process, and the idea will be explored in greater detail in Chapter 9. For our purposes here it is important to note that what is being created is a virtuous circle whereby each evolutionary advance makes it that much easier to reach the next stage.

All of this is important because unless we understand the forces that are at work it can cause us to underestimate the speed at which the future will arrive. Consider the following story.

In 1974 officials at Monsanto estimated that the sequencing of a single gene would cost $150 million. By 1990 the cost had dropped somewhat, but biochemists, who had just spent the better part of a year transcribing a measly one ten-thousandth of the human genome, scoffed at the notion that by 2005 the entire human genome would be sequenced.

Craig Venter was not among them. He understood where computer processing power was headed and what it meant for gene sequencing. In fact, he was so convinced of its potential that he started his own company, Celera Genomics, to compete with the federal government's Human Genome Project. On February 12, 2001—five years ahead of a goal that only a decade earlier had seemed impossible by some very bright people—the human genome was sequenced.

More recently, in 2007 researchers announced that they had published the first draft of the Human Metabolome Project. It is the chemical equivalent of the human genome, and it catalogued the approximately 2,500 chemicals found in the human body. It is expected to give doctors and researchers a new way to identify, diagnose, and, possibly, treat disease because today doctors are estimated to sample less that 1 percent of known metabolites during routine clinical testing. This advance, too, wouldn't have been possible without the better equipment.

THE FIRST ENABLER: THE LAW FIRM OF MOORE, DICKERSON, AND METCALFE

I have already explained Moore's law (the idea that the number of transistors capable of being packed onto a computer circuit is doubling every eighteen months), but there are a few other laws that exponential executives should familiarize themselves with because they are certain to lead to equally startling advances in a variety of other fields.

In biotechnology there is something known as Dickerson's law, and it is the medical equivalent to Moore's law. Instead of the number of transistors doubling every eighteen months, however, Richard Dickerson, now a professor of biochemistry at UCLA, predicted the accelerating pace of the discovery in the field of protein structure determination. To wit, the number of protein structures solved has increased from 1 in 1961 to a modest 23 in 1977. By 2001 the figure stood at 12,000, and in mid 2007 it was stood at 44,500 and counting. (Interested parties can track the increase at *www.rcsb.org/pdb/home/home.do*.)

All this is important for the rapidly growing field of structural genomics. The more that the medical community knows about the molecular structure of proteins, the better understanding it will have of the critical role they play in human health. Our understanding of what disease is and how those diseases can be treated should grow proportionally—which is to say exponentially—as a result of this information.

As powerful as Moore's and Dickerson's laws may be, there is a third law that is playing an even larger role in the exponential economy. That is because the "law" pertains to how the flow of information and ideas is increasing exponentially. It is called Metcalfe's law, and it is named for Robert Metcalf, coinventor of the Ethernet and founder of 3Com. He stated that the value of a telecommunications network is proportional to the square of the number of users of the system.

This law is most easily understood by thinking of the fax machine. The first fax that was built, while of obvious technological merit, had no practical use. That's because it couldn't fax a document to anyone. The value only materialized after the second fax machine was created. With each additional machine thereafter, the possibilities expanded rapidly because the total number of possible connections was proportional to the square of the number of users.

Be it the telegraph, the phone, the fax, the Internet, wireless, or WiMAX, every advance in communication technology has made it more economical and more convenient to send larger amounts of information faster, to more places, and at a lower cost than the previous generation of communication technology. The end result of this law is that information, data, and new ideas are spreading at an accelerating rate.

THE SECOND ENABLER: A GROWING FLOCK OF MAVENS

A second reason technological tipping points are quickening is because of a factor that Malcolm Gladwell spells out in his book, *The Tipping Point: How Little Things Can Make a Big Difference.* Specifically, it is now easier for "mavens"—whom Gladwell also calls connectors or salesmen—to spread the benefits of a new technology or product to ever-larger audiences on a faster time scale.

Perhaps the easiest example of how technology is putting air under the wings of the maven class is the extraordinary rise of bloggers in the past few years. No Web site better captures this than *www.TechCrunch.com*, a site dedicated to tracking and highlighting the latest developments in the world of Web 2.0. The site regularly attracts 150,000 visitors a day and posts up to six different stories a day. A single positive mention can send thousands of people (many of whom are mavens themselves and will link back to the story) to the Web site of the profiled company. Alternatively, a stinging critique can cause the company's owners to scrap its existing business model and begin devising a new one.

But mavens' growing power goes beyond blogs. Through RSS (Really Simple Syndication) feeds, followers of bloggers or other news sites are now notified almost instantly about new developments. In turn, a variety of other sites, such as *www.Digg.com* and *www.del.icio.us*, make it easier for people to find and vote on what they consider to be important and useful information. Stories, postings, or ideas that receive a lot of votes or are commented on favorably by others then rise to the top of the site, bringing even more attention to the best new ideas and technologies.

All of these tools are increasing what Gladwell termed "stickiness." To the extent that better products and ideas stick, it further explains why change is accelerating.

THE THIRD ENABLER: A BETTER CODE

In 1995 the Denver International Airport opened with great fanfare. Among its most sophisticated marvels was to be its automated baggage handler. Consisting of 26 miles of steel track, 5,000 electronic eyes, 4,000 independent telecars, 400 radio receivers, and 100 computers, designers believed that this Jetson-like system of high-tech efficiency would brilliantly and swiftly orchestrate the movement of millions of pieces of luggage between the airplane and its eagerly awaiting owners.

Alas, the system failed, the system's designer, BAE Automated Systems, was liquidated, and the airport's principal airline, United, was driven into bankruptcy, in part because of its spectacular failure.

At the heart of the systems breakdown was software. But Denver International Airport is not alone in being let down by software. The IRS, FBI, and FAA have all experienced multimillion-dollar meltdowns in the past decade. Lest anyone think that problems are somehow mysteriously linked to only organizations with three letter acronyms (Denver's airport also goes by DIA), it has been estimated that for every two large software systems that are installed, one either fails or is cancelled when failure appears imminent.

But one of the beautiful things about exponential growth, however, is that it does not discriminate between technologies. In spite of all the large-scale and stunning failures, software is getting better. Researchers at the University of California, Irvine have, for instance, constructed a "text mine" that can search hundreds of thousands of old newspaper articles and find tenuous connections between disparate information. It can now do in hours what it used to take a librarian months to do. In the medical profession, a new software system called CellTracker traces the movements of proteins within a cell and now does in a half hour what it use to take twelve hours to do. And in 2006 IBM researchers demonstrated a new software program that could read two sentences from a newspaper article and then generate a third sentence.

Such advances might sound promising—and they are—but the software's real promise emerges when it is combined with other technological advances. For example, one of the primary reasons why the winner of the 2005 DARPA robotic challenge was able to increase the robot's distance of traveling safely from just 7 miles to the 132 miles in the course of a single year was because the team installed better software that allowed the robotic vehicle to learn road surface characteristics as it went along.

The implications of vastly improved software are startling. Medical doctors are now using Google to make better diagnosis, marketers and advertisers are mining data for insights that they can use to market and sell products more efficiently, and others are using algorithms to track credit card fraud. Google's founders have even publicly stated that one of their goals is to create a machine that "would understand exactly what you mean and give back exactly what you want."

More impressive still is the work of Charles Simonyi, the former chief architect of Microsoft's software, who now has his own company and is devising something called intentional software, which, if it is successful, will allow users to express their precise needs to the computer in their own language. Put another way, the users will be able to modify and guide the software's future evolution. (There is yet another law, Wirth's law, which states, only somewhat tongue-in-cheek, that software gets slower faster than hardware gets faster. It is hoped that that intentional software and other advances will soon render this law obsolete.)

THE FOURTH ENABLER: THE OPEN-SOURCE MOVEMENT

In 1995 an amateur stargazer, Thomas Bopp, burst on to the world stage and gained his fifteen minutes of fame for codiscovering the Hale-Bopp comet. In 2004 another amateur, Jay McNeil, snapped a picture of a new nebula—a gigantic cloud of dust and gas lit by a newborn star. It was billed as the first such star found by an amateur in more than a half century. Since then close to one thousand hobbyist planet hunters have joined an Internet project called Systemic and have discovered more than 200 planets in distant solar systems.

Discovering planets is a long way from the rough-and-tumble business world, but a number of businesses are picking up on the benefits of tapping into the incredible amount of knowledge and enthusiasm that exists in the brains of individuals around the world. This relatively new phenomenon—called the open-source movement—which started in earnest seven years ago when a single individual from Finland, Linus Torvalds, unleashed a real challenge to Microsoft by making software available to anyone for free to be used and improved upon—is now gaining considerable traction in everything from astronomy, advertising, and education to the creation of new toys, robots, and products.

At the heart of the open-source philosophy is the idea that by exposing almost anything to a wider audience—be it software code, a product, a problem, or even an idea—that content can be improved upon by suggestions and ideas of other individuals. By following this practice, companies around the world are tapping into an almost limitless source of free innovation.

Consider the example of Lego. A couple years back, the company introduced its Mindstorms NXT robot kit. The developers imagined that the robot had fifteen basic functions. They agreed, however, to allow their customers to hack into the system. As a result, creative robotic enthusiasts have since concocted more than 1,000 additional things that these robots can do. Sean Adams, the founder of Slim Devices, a young start-up that manufactures products that can download digital music from a variety of sources, has done the same thing, and his customers have helped him design a better device.

Even PepsiCo and General Motors, during the 2007 Super Bowl—the granddaddy of events for TV commercials—ran open-source commercials that were written and produced by customers. According to the public's reaction after the game, the commercials fared as well as, if not better than, many of the professionally produced ads. As more companies embrace open-source thinking, the net effect will be an explosion of innovative new ideas and products.

THE FIFTH ENABLER: MONEY MAKES THE WORLD GO ROUND

Money makes the world go around, or so it is said. I don't know where this statement came from, but it probably dates back to at least Christopher Columbus's time. It might surprise you to know, though, that Columbus did not gain rapid approval for his expedition, nor did he come by the financial resources for his adventures easily. The famed explorer was rejected at least three times—by the king of Portugal, the duke of Medina-Sedonia, and the count of Medina-Celi—before finally the winning approval from the king and queen of Spain.

It is still difficult to obtain money, but for bright, motivated people with good ideas there is plenty of money to be found. To this end, many of the exponential advances outlined in the previous chapters are now being funded by large corporations with deep pockets. For instance, IBM has large initiatives underway in both supercomputing and brain scanning. Toyota and Honda are committing sizeable resources toward the development of robotics, and Intel, BASF, and GE are funding multimillion-dollar nanotechnology initiatives.

Venture capitalists are also investing considerable sums in promising biotechnology and renewable energy start-ups, and, of course, universities and the federal governments are all making strategic investments in myriad emerging technologies.

But even all of this money isn't enough for some. In recent years there has been an explosion of individuals and foundations willing to grant large cash prizes to individuals or companies capable of achieving certain technological milestones. One of the better and more recent examples is the Ansari X Prize, which awarded $10 million to Burt Rutan and Jim Benson in 2004 for becoming the first individuals to build a private space vehicle capable of carrying three people 100 kilometers above the earth, return, then repeat the trick within two weeks.

The foundation is now offering similar prizes for the first person or group to sequence 100 human genomes in ten days and another prize to whoever can produce an automobile capable of getting 100 miles per gallon.

In early 2007 Richard Branson, the founder of Virgin Airlines, got into the act by offering a $25 million prize to anyone who could develop a technology capable of taking 1 billion pounds of carbon dioxide out of the environment. On a slightly more business-oriented level, NetFlix is offering a $1 million prize for anyone who can create an algorithm that improves the accuracy of its movie recommendation service.

THE SIXTH ENABLER: THE COMPETITIVE SPIRIT

The X Prize and Branson's $25 million offering, as motivating as they may be, are just facilitating an even greater enabler—competition. People are by their nature competitive. They are also ambitious, attracted to making money and fame, and many are driven to make a mark on the world by leaving it a better place. Sometimes they are motivated by just one factor, sometimes all four—plus some other hidden motivation. Regardless, competition, like the other forces, appears to be growing exponentially as well.

A case in point involves the two principal partners of the SpaceShipOne's successful suborbital flight, Burt Rutan and Jim Benson. Just days after claiming the $10 million X Prize, the two began bickering over which man contributed more to the plane's success. To make a long story short, the two are now funding their own separate initiatives in an attempt to become the first person to establish a profitable space tourism business. Regardless of who wins, the public will be the ultimate beneficiary because the rivalry could well result in space travel for ordinary citizens being one step closer to reality.

For a slightly more tangible marker of the growing tenacity of competition, I submit the shrinking average life of a company on the S&P 500 index. In 1950 major companies could expect to survive, on average, to early adulthood—or about thirty years. Today less than half of all companies celebrate their sweet sixteenth. The median age of an S&P 500 company is now fifteen years and dropping.

No company has better exemplified the growing competitiveness of the commercial marketplace in the past few years than Google. It has forced newer companies such as Yahoo, Microsoft,

Amazon, and eBay to adjust their strategies and caused a number of traditional businesses in the advertising, newspaper, and publishing industries to radically revamp their business models.

But even Google is not safe from the long arms of competition. Near the end of 2006, Jimmy Wales, the founder of Wikipedia, announced that his for-profit company, Wikia Inc., was starting a project dubbed Wikiasari to go head-to-head with Google's computer-based algorithmic search engine.

It should be a battle for the ages. Google's algorithms will continue to get better, but Wikiasari intends to employ an open-source model that relies on the editorial judgment of humans to improve its search capabilities. Essentially it is counting on *you* to create a better search engine.

Will it work? Who knows. The end result of the competition, though, will be better search engines in large part because of the last and most important enabler—the growing power of the human mind.

THE SEVENTH ENABLER: MIND WIDE OPEN

At the beginning of 2007, the Massachusetts Institute of Technology—one of the most prestigious universities in the world—announced that by the end of the year it would put the contents of all 1,800 of its courses online for free. With this single decision, suddenly people anywhere in the world with access to a computer will be able to avail themselves of not only an almost unlimited amount of knowledge, but they will also be able to gain access to the time and talent of some of the world's best professors to help them better understand that information.

Some might argue that because so many people around the world still won't have access to a computer the offer won't have that much of an impact, but as a result of efforts such as Nicholas Negroponte's $100 computer (a program designed to supply many in the developing world with inexpensive laptop computers)—not to mention falling computer prices—this problem will be addressed over time. Still others might be inclined to dismiss the value of the effort because much of the information will be in English and thus inaccessible to non-English speakers, but here again translational software is constantly improving, and the day is not far off when MIT's contents will be quickly, cheaply, and accurately be translated into Mandarin, Farsi, French, or any other language for that matter.

In fact, by 2009, as a result of exponential advances in software, the U.S. Army, which is already employing IBM's speech-to-speech translational programs in Iraq to allow U.S. military personnel to converse with Iraqi citizens, expects the tools to be 90 percent as effective as the best human interpreter. In short, it won't be long before 300 million Chinese and 300 million Indian students have access to a free MIT, Yale, or Notre Dame education in their native language.

The people who avail themselves of this knowledge won't be able to obtain formal degrees, but if one applies the power of zenzizenzizenzic to education and jumps the curve to the year 2015, just how important will a formal diploma be in a world where half of everything a person learns in her first year of college will be obsolete by the time she graduates?

The broader point is that in the future it will matter less whether a person has an actual diploma or not. What will matter is that people can demonstrate they have the knowledge to be fully functioning members of tomorrow's global economy. Recall that many of today's biggest contributors—people such as Bill

Gates, Steve Jobs, and Michael Dell—all felt obtaining a formal education was more of a hindrance than a help to them.

In the exponential economy, a Malaysian Bill Gates, a Hungarian Steve Jobs, and a Brazilian Michael Dell are probably tapping into the wealth of information that is already online to help them bring their new ideas and products to the market.

CONCLUSION

To give you some sense of the speed at which these enablers are moving, let us return to the Wikipedia example from Chapter 2. In the week that I began writing this chapter, IBM announced the development of its new speech-to-speech translation system and China lifted its ban on Wikipedia.

The effect of the latter is that the number of Chinese users registering to contribute to the site jumped 200 percent to 1,200 people in just the first day. The effect of the former is that even if someone in Beijing posts an entry to Wikipedia in Chinese, it won't be long before his contributions will be translated into English for the English-speaking world to use. Of course, the process works both ways, so the Chinese and the rest of the world will also have access to the exponential amount of new information that others are adding to the site.

The net effect of all of this activity is the equivalent of pouring fuel on an already raging fire. To keep from getting burned, you'll need to learn how to jump the curve. But before one can effectively jump the curve, it will first help to know how to walk the escalator.

All mankind is divided into three classes: those who immoveable, those who are moveable, and those who move.

—Benjamin Franklin

There is no elevator to success. You have to take the stairs.

—Anonymous

CHAPTER 4

Walk the Escalator

Go to any shopping mall, office complex, or airport where there is an escalator and observe the number of people who are content to allow this twentieth-century wonder carry them to their destination without having to lift a foot. It is difficult to imagine that this is what Jesse Reno had in mind when he patented his "inclined elevator," or how Charles Seeberger, who later redesigned the device and coined the term escalator, envisioned it being used.

Rather, I suspect, they viewed the escalator as a way to help those who were not able to move well, such as the elderly and infirm, or perhaps as a method for facilitating pedestrian traffic among the more able bodied. One wonders if they might be a distressed to learn that a century later their invention is sometimes slowing the pace of things. Nevertheless, this is what has come to pass.

The escalator can be viewed as a metaphor for many of today's extraordinary technologies which can do many remarkable things and make us faster and more productive—provided we view them as tools to assist us rather than as a means to avoid all effort.

To take the analogy one step further, people must learn to "walk the escalator." Put another way: Before one can hope to jump the curve to the next level, it helps to get a running—or in this case, at least, a walking—start by better utilizing existing technology.

Exponential **INSIGHT**

Randy Moss, the star football wide receiver who played for the Minnesota Vikings for some time, used to boast that he would use the huge Jumbotron screen in the Metrodome to alert him to when his quarterback had released the ball. He claimed this information gave him an advantage over his defensive opponent. I can't verify the veracity of the statement, but it gets at the idea of how an existing technology can be used to one's benefit.

A more pertinent example is the Metropolitan Opera. In late 2006 the Met began broadcasting live performances to different venues. By using HDTV and digital technology, the Met showed one single performance in 100 theaters to more than 30,000 people. At an average ticket price of $18, the Metropolitan Opera generated a quick $540,000 in new revenue by simply employing an existing technology. Whether you're looking to score or just broadcast the benefits of a new product, a number of existing technologies can help you do your job better today.

JUMP THE CURVE STRATEGY #3:
Look to the Kindness of Strangers

The notion of building a better product—a better mousetrap, if you will—is a powerful one, and more often than not the central figure in the story has been the lone individual who is frequently portrayed as diligently laboring away in his basement or garage devising a new or improved product. The importance of individual skill, initiative, knowledge, and capability will always remain important, but a new dynamic is now growing in power and it lies outside of domain of the individual. If one replaces the term mousetrap with mountain bike, this idea becomes clearer.

It may surprise you to learn that the popular off-road mountain bike wasn't invented by a single person toiling away in his garage. Rather the bike morphed over time as a variety of committed, dedicated, and passionate cyclists began tinkering with their bikes to help them better meet the stringent requirements of their off-road pursuits.

First someone decided that the bike should have large balloon tires to better withstand the rough terrain. This was followed by thumb-shifting derailleur gears to allow bikers to more easily navigate steep mountain slopes. Next came motorcycle lever-operated drum brakes (to better stop while moving downhill), and eventually flat handlebars and lightweight tubing were added to confer additional advantages.

The lesson in this story is twofold. First, products evolve. Secondly, evolutionary advances are often developed by the people who rely on the product and not employees of the company manufacturing the product. There is nothing new or radical in this idea, but today's technology has now sufficiently advanced to the stage where businesses can do a much better job of reaching out to those users to harness their ideas and speed up the evolutionary progression of their products.

At the forefront of this trend is the open-source movement. Several examples of this movement have already been cited in Chapter 3. To fully understand the potential of the open-source movement, however, we will focus on something tangible: gold.

In 2002 GoldCorp's CEO, Rob McEwen, wasn't fully convinced that, in spite of what his company's experts were telling him, there wasn't more gold to be mined in his company's main Red Lake mine.

To test his hunch, he proposed to do something radical. He wanted to open up his company's geological data—which in the gold industry is a closely held proprietary secret—to the world's most knowledgeable mining experts and give them a chance to determine if there might be more gold in the mine. As an incentive, McEwen offered a sizeable financial prize to anyone who could make a compelling case as to why his company should look for gold in a particular location. If the person's hypotheses proved correct, he or she would be awarded the money.

Over the objections of his board of directors, McEwen posted his company's information on the Internet. Within days the Web site generated 500,000 hits, and 1,400 people from over fifty countries entered submissions. The company then selected the five best entries and began mining. Goldcorp struck gold on four of five selections. Today the company has increased its market capitalization almost fourfold, and Red Lake mine remains one of the world's more profitable gold mines.

There is no shortage of other companies tapping into the open-source movement. Lego and iRobot, the maker of the robotic

Roomba vacuum cleaner, are allowing their best customers to see and experiment with early beta versions of products, and they are listening to their suggestions about how to improve these products. IBM is opening up its patents to outside lawyers and even its competitors in an effort to speed up the patent-approval process, and Proctor & Gamble and a handful number of pharmaceutical companies are using a Web site called *InnoCentive.com* to post some of their more intractable problems in the hopes of tapping into the expertise that exists within the broader research community.

Exponential INSIGHT

Right out of college I served as a naval intelligence officer and was privy to classified photos from supersecret satellites flying above the earth. Today anyone can go to Google Earth and download comparable photos.

What is more interesting is that with this information citizen-sleuths are now making discoveries that have eluded even the best intelligence analysts. In 2006 the Associated Press published a story about a man who had a passion for viewing Chinese landscape. One day he discovered a peculiar topographical feature in a remote corner of northwest China. Something looked familiar about it, but he couldn't put his finger on it. Eventually he realized the site was identical to a strategic piece of real estate along the Sino-Indian border. From this he correctly deduced that China had replicated the territory to better practice attacks against the target in India. In the exponential economy, secrets might actually yield more value by being declassified.

In fact, back in 2000, P&G, which has a large research and development staff of 8,000, announced an ambitious goal of having half of its new products and technologies come from outside the company. Seven years into the initiative, the company reports that 35 percent of all new products bear at least some input from outsiders. Moreover, it reports that productivity of its in-house staff has increased by 60 percent.

JUMP THE CURVE STRATEGY #4:
Just "Wiki" It

The earlier point about how P&G has increased its productivity speaks to another new mechanism that can increase productivity: wikis. Established on the premise that all of us together are smarter than any of us individually, wikis provide a powerful tool for helping companies collaborate on projects, manage group information, and incubate ideas on an accelerated basis.

The concept has grown so popular that even the process of writing of books is being wiki-fied. In the fall of 2006, I accepted an invitation to participate in the writing of a book entitled *We Are Smarter Than Me*, which attempts to demonstrate that a community can write a more compelling book than an individual expert.

I can't say I contributed anything terribly profound, but I did add the following example to the chapter on open-source ideas:

Scott Adams and *Dilbert*. In 1998, Scott Adams, the creator of the comic strip *Dilbert*, became the first cartoonist to publish his e-mail address in his carton strip. Whether it was by strategic intent or dumb luck, Adams now regularly supplements his comic strip—which chronicles bureaucratic absurdities, management ineptitude, and bouts of corporate stupidity—with poignant insights and stories from his legions of fans who send him more than one thousand e-mails a day. From this pool of ideas, Adams has been able to augment his own extraordinary creativity to create more cartoon strips, and he also draws on the public's input to provide better content for his books, Web site, and blog.

Whether it will be accepted, modified, or deleted is now in the hands of the community. The more intriguing result will be if the project works and the community creates a compelling book. My hunch is that it will because wikis offer an easy-to-use mechanism for tapping into a wider base of knowledge. Wikis also allow ideas to be shared, modified, amended, and otherwise improved on a faster basis than any conventional system.

One company that is employing a wiki with some success today is GlaxoSmithKline, which uses one to allow employees to share information during clinical trials for its new drugs. By providing people with the opportunity to supply their colleagues with more context, updated information, and even advice, the company's management is using the wiki to help GlaxoSmith-Kline successfully avoid traps and pitfalls that have hindered it in the past. The net impact is that faulty drug candidates are being pulled quicker, and successful ones are reaching market sooner because regulators' questions and concerns are being addressed in greater detail at an earlier stage. The former outcome saves the company money; the latter helps it make new money.

Exponential INSIGHT

It is often hard for employees to be productive when cowork-ers constantly interrupt them with questions. A wiki can minimize such disruptions by allowing employees to create an ongoing database of common information. Questions and answers can be posted directly to the site where they can even be given more contextual depth. For instance, com-ments can be left and related Web sites and documents can be hyperlinked into a wiki. As more people begin contribut-ing increasing amounts of information to the wiki, the utility and value of it will increase proportionately.

JUMP THE CURVE STRATEGY #5:
Bet On It

In the summer of 2003, members of the United States Congress went apoplectic when news broke of the Defense Advanced Research Projects Agency's (DARPA) program to help predict terrorist attacks and assassinations by allowing people to bet money on the likelihood of such events. (DARPA is the central research and development organization for the Department of Defense.) There is, of course, something unseemly about wager-ing on a tragedy, but what is ironic is that such systems have proven remarkably successful at predicting a variety of outcomes because people's financial interests are appropriately aligned with accurately assessing the odds of the event occurring. Thus, prop-erly used, the system could help prevent the very thing that Con-gress wanted to stop from happening.

The program was terminated, but a number of companies, including Google, Pfizer, and Microsoft, now regularly make use of such systems to allow employees to make bets on the outcome of everything from when a product might launch or assessing the prospects that a particular department will meets it quarterly sales goals to determining whether a new TV commercial will be a hit.

What is unique about such systems is that managers receive a different type of information than they might ordinarily receive from their subordinates. For example, a few years ago a Microsoft business manager kept telling her boss that a product was on schedule to launch on time. When the boss inquired why so many of the manager's own employees were betting that the product wouldn't launch until the following year, the manager was forced to admit that the program had run into hurdles. As a result, additional resources were committed to the project and, while the project was still late, Microsoft was at least able to get it to the market faster than otherwise would have been the case because of the unique insight that the market-based system afforded company managers.

Exponential INSIGHT

Managers are, of course, encouraged to always listen to their employees' words, but frequently what employees are saying is vastly differently than what their money is saying. By creating a system that aligns their financial interests with the company's, managers can glean some useful information.

JUMP THE CURVE STRATEGY #6:
Let the Computer Do It

The incredible power of today's supercomputers has already been discussed in some detail in Chapter 2. These behemoths are large and expensive to operate. As such, their potential might seem out of reach for the average small to medium-size business.

This is true to a degree, but there are ways around the problem. Companies such as Amazon.com, which in 2006 introduced its Elastic Compute Cloud initiative, have begun to address this issue and are now renting access to massive computing power for about 10 cents per CPU hour. This means that 700 CPUs can be had for as little as $70.

In practical terms, this means a one-time problem that could benefit from having a few billion calculations run on its behalf can now be done fairly easily. IBM is also beginning to make supercomputing available to the masses.

One firm that took advantage of IBM's program potential was SmartOps, a small company specializing in inventory optimization for other companies. It had a problem that involved over 70,000 SKUs (stock keeping units). Running the problem with a regular computer would have taken six hours, but with the help of an IBM supercomputer the problem was solved in seventeen seconds. The task proved so efficient that the company began to experiment with how other variables might impact the inventory, and quickly it was able to construct an even better solution.

If renting such computing power is still beyond your means, there is, again, the kindness of strangers. It might amaze you to know that the amount of computing power sitting idle in America at any given moment is the equivalent of thousands of supercomputers. Innovative organizations and individuals are now tapping into this power by asking people to use their computers when the owners are not using them.

The best known example is SETI@home, which is using over 1.2 million home computers to process signals from outer space in its search for intelligent life. A slightly more down-to-earth application can be found in the example of David Baker, a professor of biochemistry at the University of Washington, who is "walking the escalator" and is using distributed computing to search for a cure for cancer.

After his wife was diagnosed with cancer, Baker began looking for a solution to her problem. To pursue his research he realized that he needed an incredible amount of computing power. Not being a wealthy man, he put his request for computing assistance out on the Internet. Today he has more than 60,000 computers toiling away on his behalf, and he hopes to increase the number tenfold in the future.

To benefit from this approach, one doesn't always need access to ten of thousands of computers. In the spring of 2006, Stefan Krah, an amateur code breaker, was occupied with cracking an old, unbroken Nazi code from World War II. Like Baker, Krah laid out his problem on the Internet and explained why he needed some extra computing power. Within a day he had five computers, and shortly thereafter 2,500 people had deemed his project of enough interest that they allowed Krah to use their computers. In almost no time, the computers quickly ran through 150 million permutations and cracked the code. All it revealed was the location of a long decommissioned (or destroyed) German submarine, but one can see the potential of the application of distributed computing for science and business in the next decade.

Exponential **INSIGHT**

Searching for extraterrestrials and deciphering old World War II codes may not be on the top of everyone's agenda. However, the fact that people are pursuing such tasks and, more importantly, that thousands of people are willing to open their computers to help find the solution indicates that not possessing a supercomputer is an insufficient reason for standing on the escalator. Who knows? By tapping into the power of computers you just might find something that is out of this world or discover a small secret that could help you in your next battle with your competitors.

JUMP THE CURVE STRATEGY #7:
Reorganize Your Data Storage Closet

At the time this book went to press, Apple's most recent iPod was capable of storing 80 gigabytes—or approximately 20,000 songs. Assuming that one had the all free time to listen to that much music—and a person very well may if she or he has a daily commute in one of the major cities of world—it would take that person just over a month, listening nonstop, to work his way through every song. Regardless of whether such a scenario is closer to your idea of heaven or hell, I think we can all agree that storing 80 GB of data on a device about the size of hotel-sized bar of soap is, for now, an impressive accomplishment.

Of course, this much data can be used for things besides just listening to music or downloading a recent episode of *Desperate Housewives*. A number of businesses are already using this capacity to walk the escalator by redesigning and retooling basic business operations.

In 2006, Siemens, the giant German-based conglomerate, purchased all of its medical technicians mp3 players at a cost of $30,000. By the end of the year it had reaped an eightfold return on its investment by cutting in half the number of training sessions it had to hold for those employees. (The cost per training session was $125,000.) More importantly, the mp3 players are being used to help ensure Siemen's employees stay abreast of the latest advances in their field by downloading and listening to relevant podcasts.

Data storage is by no means limited to mp3 players. Safely and securely housing vast amounts of financial, marketing, and personnel and customer information is a chore, especially for smaller companies. Here again, a number of organizations are walking the escalator by outsourcing this task to companies that have mastered the data storage business. For instance, Amazon and Seagate are both now offering businesses of almost every size the ability to store and retrieve any amount of information, at any time, from anywhere on the Web. The systems are fast, reliable, scalable, and have the added benefit of allowing smaller businesses to dispense with the cost and overhead for the personnel and equipment that are necessary to handle such responsibilities.

JUMP THE CURVE STRATEGY #8:
Run the Numbers

I am going to predict that the 2008 NBA champions will be the Houston Rockets. I don't do this out of loyalty for the Rockets—

I'm a fan of the Minnesota Timberwolves. Instead it is because the Rockets' new management team is subjecting its entire roster to the power of quantitative analysis.

Quantitative analysis in professional sports is nothing new. It was the subject of Michael Lewis's best-selling book, *Moneyball*, and has been cited by baseball experts as the reason why the Oakland A's, in spite of having one of the lowest payrolls in professional baseball, are consistently among the league's better teams.

Quantitative analysis is even credited with helping the 2004 Boston Red Sox break the Curse of the Bambino and end its eighty-six-year-old quest to win the World Series. Both teams' general managers, Oakland's Billy Beane and Boston's Theo Epstein, admit to regularly using quantitative analysis to determine everything from how a trade for a particular player will impact the team's on-field performance to where a certain player should be inserted in the batting rotation on any given day.

Translating baseball's more linear nature—where it is relatively straightforward to isolate a player's individual performance by discerning the difference between, say, a single and a home run—is far easier than figuring out the relative value of a basketball player. This is due to the complex ways in which a basketball team's five players interact with one another while on the court. For instance, is a basket more valuable than the assist that made it possible? What about the value of a rebound as opposed to a blocked shot? And which has more impact on a game's outcome, a player's ability to steal two passes a game or his skill in consistently setting good picks?

These have been vexing questions, but economists have now developed an algorithm to help measure a player's "wins produced" for his team, and the Rocket's general-manager-in-waiting, Carroll Dawson, (who will officially take the reins as GM at the beginning of the 2007–08 season), has an MBA from MIT's Sloan School of Management and is applying these algorithms to select the players he believes will best help his team win.

To this end, one of the reasons the Rockets signed former Duke standout Shane Battier had little to do with his 10.1 points per game average or his high shooting percentage (.488); it had more to do with his rebounds per game, his dramatic defensive ability, and his skill at quickly moving the ball around to his open teammates.

Time will tell if my prediction about the Houston Rockets will pan out, but the net effect of this emphasis on algorithms is that it is helping a number of businesses make better decisions today. For instance, Shell Oil is using complicated mathematical algorithms to help determine where to drill for oil, and it likely played a leading role in assisting Chevron scientists locate that company's new massive Jack2 oil discovery in the Gulf of Mexico in the fall of 2006. And with Google Trends, businesses of all sizes can analyze and better understand how, where, and by whom its products are being used.

Exponential **INSIGHT**

Whether you're looking to improve your on-base percentage, take your game to a new level, or just find a new discovery, crunching the numbers can yield some surprising findings.

JUMP THE CURVE STRATEGY #9:
Follow Your Hunch

Supreme Court Justice Potter Stewart once famously observed when commenting about pornography, "I'll know it when I see it." Unwittingly, Stewart was elucidating a problem that has plagued computer scientists for years. Computers, for all of their incredible power and capabilities, are nowhere as good as humans at discerning faces, judging beauty, and, if need be, telling someone what may or may not be pornographic.

Now researchers are marrying the power of computers to the pattern-recognizing skills of humans in order to design better products. The simplest way to think of this is to consider a nice photo of yourself but one that is perhaps slightly out of focus and suffers from poor lighting. Photoshop and a number of other software packages provide the tools to improve the photo, but they require that the user be familiar with hues, gamma corrections, and other assorted tools. All the average person knows is that she wants the photo to look better.

With "hunch" software, a series of mutated photos would appear on the screen with different adjustments in focus and lightening, and the user can then select the photo that appears best. The process continues until the photo is refined to the person's preference.

The beauty of this approach is that the users don't have to know anything about photo software, nor do they even have to describe what precisely they are looking for. Like Justice Stewart, they will just know the best photo when they see it.

This technology is still in its infancy, but such software is already being used by researchers at pharmaceutical companies, who are using their "hunches" to select certain molecules that might make promising drug candidates. (The computer then recombines the molecule into a series of other mutated molecules in the hopes that it will bring them one step closer to an effective drug.) Home decorating stores are also using the technology to assist customers select color patterns and room layouts that are more to their liking by allowing them to continually refine the colors until they find the ones most suitable to their tastes.

The technology, however, goes well beyond these limited applications. For example, few people can describe precisely what they want in a car, a Web site, or clothing, but they will know what they like when they see it. To this end, Amazon.com now offers a tool to help businesses do this. It is called the Mechanical Turk, and the company calls it "*artificial* artificial intelligence," because it uses human intelligence to improve computer intelligence.

Exponential **INSIGHT**

If you have a hunch that you should be employing more technology but are not yet convinced that machines do a lot of things as well as a person, you're correct. But new tools do now exist that can help increase the performance of both man and machine.

JUMP THE CURVE STRATEGY #10:
Get in Touch with All of Your Sensors

In November 2006 two events took place that suggest sensor technology is nearing a tipping point. First, Mothers Against Drunk Driving (MADD) announced a plan to install sensor technology in the car of anyone convicted of driving under the influence of alcohol. The organization's rationale was that in spite of the great progress it has made in the past two decades since it began pushing for tougher laws against drunk drivers, statistics indicated that in recent years the number of deaths caused by drunk drivers has stayed steady. MADD wanted to do better and it believed sensor technology could help.

After the proposal was announced, proponents believed it would still be years before the technology had matured and dropped in price to a point where the major automobile manufacturers would consider installing it. In early 2007 Toyota surprised observers by announcing that it was actively developing the technology and felt such sensors could be installed as early as 2008. Obviously there are privacy concerns surrounding the technology as well as legitimate issues about how people—especially serial drunk driving offenders—might get around it, but Toyota's announcement proves that sensor technology is now practical enough to be seriously considered for such applications.

The second event took place in Britain when Marks & Spencer, the larger British retailer, announced that it had achieved its goal of 100 percent stock accuracy, following its successful trial of employing RFID tags in forty-two stores to track inventory. The company added that it planned to increase that number to eighty stores by the end of 2007. (By embedding the RFID tags in throwaway wrappers and not the product themselves, Marks & Spencer was able to adroitly sidestep the privacy issue.)

Exponential **INSIGHT**

In today's global environment, low-cost sensors and RFID tags have the potential to imbue old products with new capabilities as well as give retailers and others a real advantage in terms of managing inventory. In businesses where the margins are already razor thin, these small tools could make a big difference. To return to the "better mousetrap" idea, it might surprise you to know that the latest and greatest mousetrap is now armed with a sensor that alerts homeowners whenever a rodent has been snared. In addition to freeing people from having to unnecessarily check the devices, the sensors are also useful in better determining where the mice are coming from.

JUMP THE CURVE STRATEGY #11:
Park n' Save With Robots

If you have ever lived, worked in, or visited New York City and had to get around by car, you understand what a hassle parking can be. You might be happy to learn that in early 2007 a company opened a new robotic parking garage. What makes the system so special—besides the fact that you no longer have to relinquish the keys to your new sports car to a testosterone-charged teenager—is that the system is so efficient that it can fit sixty-seven cars in a space that previously held only twenty-four. It is able to pull off this feat by packing cars closer to one another (there is no need to leave space to open a car door) and by doing away with ramps and other superfluous maneuvering space. When you consider that it costs roughly $25 a day to park in New York City and multiply that figure by the number of additional cars such a system can handle, it provides some modest idea of how robots can help some businesses walk the escalator.

All across the field of robotics, similar opportunities for cost savings are emerging. Robotic vacuum cleaners and floor scrubbers are helping building maintenance companies cut down on janitorial costs, and the military is now employing robots to disarm roadside bombs and patrol dangerous areas. As mentioned earlier, robots are now performing 35 percent of all prostatectomies.

Less understood is that these robotic systems are so good at what they do that patients often have significantly shorter recovery times due to the precision and delicacy with which the robots perform the surgical operation. In more practical terms, this means shorter hospitals stays and fewer nurses to watch over the patients. It also suggests that hospitals can free up more doctors, nurses, and beds to serve other needier patients.

Exponential **INSIGHT**

Whether you are looking to squeeze a little more efficiency out of an existing operation, fighting a new battle, or are just trying to clean up around the office better, a growing number of robots are available to walk the escalator with you.

JUMP THE CURVE STRATEGY #12:
Think Small . . . Really Small

The term nanotechnology often brings to mind *Star Trek* episodes or conjures up futuristic images of nanobots patrolling our bloodstream in search of deadly cancer cells. While such nanobot-like devices are, in fact, under development, the reality of nano-technology is, for the time being, slightly more prosaic. The profits it is producing, though, are not, and a number of companies are employing nanotechnology to walk the escalator today.

Nano-Tex, a manufacturer of nanofibers, has been treating, among other things, the pants of Eddie Bauer, Lee Jeans, and Perry Ellis for almost four years now. The company's nano-whiskers, as they are called, infuse the pants with amazing stain-resistant properties. Since 2004, when it treated 20 million pair of pants, the company has now increased that total to an estimated 100 million enhanced garments.

Nano-Tex and other companies are also treating upholstery and carpeting with nanoparticles, and hotel and restaurant chains are using these fabrics to reduce cleaning bills and limit the frequency with which they have to replace furniture. According to Wilbur Ross, the owner of Nano-Tex, sales of nano-enhanced textiles will grow from $11 billion in 2007 to $120 billion in 2011.

Another industry using nanotechnology today is the paint and coating industry, which employs nanoparticles to create self-cleaning and scratch-resistant paints. In one interesting example, DuPont has teamed up with a small nanotechnology company, Ecology Coatings, to create something called a "liquid solid." Because the coating can be applied so thinly and so quickly, it is expected to cut the material and energy-related costs of painting automobiles by 75 percent and 25 percent, respectfully. As an added benefit, because the nanoparticles also eliminate the use of industrial solvents, it removes the need for the company to obtain environmental permits and comply with certain costly regulations.

Almost everywhere one turns these days, the advances of nanotechnology can be spotted. In 2005 the Food and Drug Administration approved the first drug using nanoparticles; in 2006 Nanosolar, a company using nanoparticles to manufacture a new thin-film solar cell, broke ground on a massive manufacturing facility; and in 2007 IBM and Intel both announced that they would be reformulating their recipe for silicon at the atomic level to improve the speed of existing computer chips by 20 percent while also cutting down on energy consumption by a factor of ten.

Exponential INSIGHT

The application of the smallest of sciences can lead to some very big improvements in product performance—and profits. For instance, self-cleaning windows and materials can help a number of companies cut down on maintenance costs, and better-insulating nanomaterials can cut down on a business's energy consumption. Alternatively, nanotechnology can adversely impact a number of existing businesses. Consider the impact on the dry-cleaning business as billions of garments begin to be coated with stain-resistant nanofibers or the impact of scratch-resistant paints on both the automobile repair business and the insurance industry. If you operate in an industry where the profits are razor thin, the emerging science of the small—nanotechnology—might be able to protect and pad those margins.

JUMP THE CURVE STRATEGY #13:
Catch a Wave

On January 26, 2006, a NASA satellite flying in geosynchronous orbit detected hurricane-force winds developing in the North Pacific. Using supercomputers, officials at the National Oceanic and Atmospheric Administration predicted that massive waves would reach Half Moon Bay, California, on February 7. Organizers at Mavericks, the world famous surfing location, sponsored a surfing contest, and officials at NBC agreed to cover the event live.

The humongous waves arrived as predicted. Using a proprietary wireless mesh network and cameras with 70x zoom lenses, NBC then sent those signals over a fiber-optic cable to the parking lot in Mavericks where thousands of fans watched the surfers ply their trade on a gigantic plasma screen. Hundreds of thousands more watched the action live on the Web via video stream that was transmitted with a directional antenna. As if that weren't enough, NBC later aired the footage on the 7,000-square-foot screen in Times Square so that the citizens of the Big Apple could gain an appreciation of the actual size of the waves that confronted the surfers that day.

The story is a wonderful example of using existing technology to walk the escalator. But just as the waves of Half Moon Bay grew exponentially larger prior to breaking, so too are all of the aforementioned technologies. To survive in tomorrow's exponential economy will require more than just walking the escalator. It will require running very fast and jumping extraordinarily high to survive.

With that in mind then, let us return to a time when running and jumping were part of our daily routine—our childhood. As you will see, many of the skills we left behind from that era will have to be relearned in order to effectively jump the curve.

Imagination is more important than knowledge. For knowledge is limited to all we now know and understand, while imagination embraces the entire world, and all there ever will be to know and understand.

—Albert Einstein

Sit down before fact as a little child, be prepared to give up every preconceived notion, follow humbly wherever and to whatever abyss nature leads, or you shall learn nothing.

—Thomas Huxley

CHAPTER 5

The Power of Play

A couple of years ago, just after turning forty, my wife asked me what I would like for Christmas. Normally I stumble over such questions, but this year I knew exactly what I wanted: juggling balls.

"Like the kind you might see a little kid playing with?" she asked.

"Exactly," I responded with all the enthusiasm of five-year-old sitting on Santa's lap.

"Okay," she replied, shrugging her shoulders. I think she was just relieved that while my midlife crisis was decidedly juvenile in nature, at least it was an inexpensive crisis—no expensive convertible sports car or fancy big-screen plasma TV.

"Don't you want to know why I want juggling balls?" I inquired.

She could see from the twinkle in my eye that I was dying to tell her, so to humor me she replied, "Why?"

"Because I just read an article that said that 95 percent of everything we have learned about the human brain we have learned in the just the past twenty years. Isn't that extraordinary?"

Impatiently, she said, "I thought you were going to tell me why you wanted juggling balls for Christmas."

"I was," I replied, undaunted. "Beginning jugglers can increase the volume of their grey matter by more than 3 percent according to a study I just read." Continuing on in the expectation that this might not sufficiently impress her, I gushed, "Other studies have suggested that juggling may actually increase creativity by causing your brain neurons to fire in new ways."

Figuring my head could probably use a little retooling, she granted me my Christmas wish, and for the better part of Christmas Eve I recused myself from my in-laws and practiced juggling.

The task started easily enough as I followed the directions, which told me to practice with just one ball until I had mastered tossing it in a perfect arc from one hand to the other. Having accomplished that within a minute, I next added a second ball to my repertoire, and not long afterward I was tossing two balls back and forth with the grace of an acrobat.

I was now ready to juggle, or so I thought. The task of adding the third ball was far more difficult than I had imagined. I finally had to give up Christmas Eve—actually it was 1:30 A.M. Christmas morning when my wife pleaded with me to come to bed because she knew our children would be waking in a few hours to see what Santa had delivered.

Neuroscientists have since offered me an explanation for my compulsive behavior that evening as well as the following day when I spent about as much time practicing my juggling as I did playing with my children. Some scientists speculate that when we attempt to learn something new, certain chemicals are released as our brain tries to establish new neural pathways. In the right doses, these chemicals can create a pleasurable sensation. These good feelings create a kind of positive feedback loop. (They also helped me persist in the face of hundreds of dropped balls.)

To this day, I can still recall the satisfaction I felt upon finally juggling the three balls with some consistency. Alas, almost as quickly as my own kids grew bored with their gifts, I, too, grew bored with juggling. I can and still do juggle on occasion, but it no longer provides that early feeling of euphoria. Part of the reason is that the neural pathways necessary to perform the task have now been wired, and there is no need for any chemicals to be released.

The point of this story is that the feeling of euphoria that accompanied my learning something new is analogous to what a young child feels on an almost daily basis as he or she is first experiencing and learning about the new world. Children, it has been estimated, begin their life with approximately 1 quadrillion synaptic connections, but as they adjust to their environment— and learn what is and isn't useful, practical, and important—they lose up to 20 billion synaptic connections a day.

The good news is that this neural plasticity does not just disappear in adults. It can be revived and reactivated, but it requires mental exercise—such as I was doing when I was learning to juggle. Therefore, this chapter is entitled the "The Power of Play," and it is all about revitalizing the connections that were so necessary for learning as young children because life in the exponential economy will require an extraordinary amount of new learning.

JUMP THE CURVE STRATEGY #14:
Stop Acting Your Age

Many adults tend to think of play as an indulgence or, worse, a frivolous waste of time. I don't know where this idea came from or when it first began creeping into popular culture, but to take advantage of the exponential economy, exponential executives must disabuse themselves of this notion.

Play has consistently been found to reduce stress, increase energy levels, brighten people's outlook, increase optimism, and foster creativity. All are worthy goals and can help individuals do their jobs better, so the question is: Why don't we play more?

I don't know the answer to that question, but play has a rich and productive history and is the basis for much of our modern economy. Long before Alexander Graham Bell uttered his famous words, "Mr. Watson—come here—I want to see you," to his assistant, he began his journey into the science of sound as a child by playing in the fields behind his family's farm where he honed his extraordinary sense of hearing by trying to listen to wheat grow. That's right, Bell would sit in the field and literally try to hear what the crop sounded like as it was growing over the summer.

One might only imagine what synaptic connections were being strengthened during this exercise, but Bell later followed up his curiosity about sound by pressing his lips up against the forehead of his mother, who was almost totally deaf, to make her bones resonate to his voice. In so doing, he found he could communicate with her. He was also now one step closer to imagining the new possibilities that carrying sound might create.

No less an exponential thinker than Albert Einstein also engaged in childlike thinking. The general theory of relatively, which has been hailed as the most important discovery of the twentieth century, came about in part because Einstein conducted a thought experiment and wondered what it would be like to ride a train through time. Few of us are as creative or brilliant as Alexander Graham Bell or Albert Einstein, but we should all heed Einstein's words about never ceasing "to stand like curious children" before the world into which we were born.

Picking up on this theme, near the end of World War II, Vannevar Bush, the science advisor to President Harry Truman, wrote a report called "Science: The Endless Frontier." The document is remarkable for a number of reasons, not the least of which is because in it Bush drew attention to the importance of supporting the "free play of intellects." He stressed that scientists and researchers must be allowed to work "on subjects of their own choosing, in a manner dictated by their curiosity for exploration."

Why did he propose this? It most certainly wasn't born out of any sense of indulgence or luxury. At the time, America was still battling Japan in the Pacific, and the outcome of World War II remained unknown.

Rather it was because Bush knew that the country would need additional breakthrough ideas in both warfare—in the event the atomic bomb didn't work (which at the time was a very real possibility)—and economics if America wanted to retain its new standing in the global economy. In short, Bush's memo to the president was not the product of an idealistic theorist; but rather that of hard-headed realist. Scientific and intellectual "play" were absolutely critical to the United States's long-term prosperity and survival.

The message is even important today. Executives and managers who feel the speed and pace of globalization dictate that they, their employees, and their companies "play" less are drawing absolutely the wrong conclusion. Play is an essential life skill.

Why are humans among the few animals that play? It has been theorized by some that play is an integral form of learning. It allows people to practice skills they might need later down the line. But play goes beyond such life skills. When we play we gain practice manipulating things and controlling the outcome of events. We also devise new solutions for old problems and create new endings for our experiences.

Exponential INSIGHT

Alan Kay once said, "The best way to predict the future is to invent it." One way to jump the curve and begin inventing new things is to return to your childhood roots and begin juggling new things around in your mind, listening for new sounds in odd places, and engaging in some old-fashioned free play. You will be surprised at the connections you make.

JUMP THE CURVE STRATEGY #15:
Mandatory Recess

A mandatory recess might not sound like a sure-fire path to prosperity, but providing employees a period of unstructured free time to pursue activities of their choosing can be very beneficial. A handful of companies have already instituted such policies. Among some of the better known companies are Google, Genentech, and 3M. All three companies have policies that allow some of their employees to spend anywhere between 15 percent and 20 percent of their time pursuing independent projects of their own choosing. In essence the companies are giving their employees permission to play.

3M has been a proponent of this practice for the longest period of time. According to company officials, the practice dates back to the 1920s when an employee reportedly disobeyed an order to abandon a project and ended up creating Scotch masking tape—one of the most successful products of all time.

One of 3M's better known and more recent success stories is that of the Post-it Note, which was developed by an employee who, because of 3M's policy, was free to pursue the project. The benefits, though, go beyond these isolated successes. 3M has an incredible history of developing new products. For years the company has publicized the fact that 50 percent of its annual revenues can be traced back to products that were developed within the past five years.

One of the reasons it has been able to regularly achieve this goal is because employees have been encouraged to innovate and have then been given the freedom to pursue new ideas. The mandatory recess policy has not only reinforced the idea that continued innovation was critical to the company's success, it has given management the confidence to stay focused on ideas that at first might have seemed either like dead ends or were too off the wall to pursue.

Another company that has embraced a discretionary time policy is Genentech. For the past few years the biotechnology company has consistently been ranked as one of the best places to work in America. There are many reasons for this, but one is because it allows its scientists discretionary time to pursue independent projects—in some cases up to 100 percent of their time. Genentech officials credit the creation of the anticancer drug Avastin—a product with over a $1 billion in annual sales—to its "discretionary time" policy.

As I explained in Chapter 2, the cost of the price of sequencing genes will continue to plummet due to the creation of ever faster computers and more sophisticated gene sequencing techniques and tools. As these things occur, not only will new drug treatments become available, but scientists and researchers are more likely to find innovative solutions to create drugs that are increasingly tailored to individual users.

Finally there is Google. In many ways, it has the boldest recess policy because it applies to *all* of the company's employees (3M's and Genentech's programs are limited to its scientific and R&D staffs). Among the programs company officials attribute to its policy are the creation of Google News Service, Orkut (its social networking site), and Gmail.

In addition to generating new innovative products, mandatory recess offers one additional benefit that is hard to quantify, but is nonetheless extremely important: It is a powerful recruiting and retention tool. There is a fierce battle to attract and retain talented workers. One of the reasons Google, Genentech, and 3M are doing as well as they are is their policies send a clear message to prospective employees: The company trusts them to pursue interesting and important projects that they believe are in the company's best long-term interests.

By giving workers this freedom, companies accrue one additional benefit. Employees now have a way of not simply meeting expectations—they have a way of surpassing them.

Exponential **INSIGHT**

If you want employees to jump the curve, you have to give them the time and space to jump. As I will continue to demonstrate throughout this book, there will be no shortage of wild ideas and strange possibilities due to exponential advances in technology. Consider just a few of the possibilities that the emerging science of nanotechnology might enable materials scientists to play around with. For instance, plastic, glass, and steel are already being made stronger, lighter, more flexible and, in some cases, self-cleaning. Soon self-healing materials, flexible electronics, and solar fabrics will be on the market. Some of these advances will lead to innovative new products and applications. Thinking up new ideas will require people to follow their hunches and, sometimes, make counterintuitive jumps in logic. Running such off-the-wall ideas by management could, at best, be difficult. Better those employees just be given some mandatory recess time to pursue their ideas.

JUMP THE CURVE STRATEGY #16:
Play with New Toys

Even if you're unwilling to provide your employees a mandatory recess, there are still other things that can be done to keep employees from acting their age. One of the better examples comes compliments of a small design company called Inventables. Over the years the company has lined up a number of big clients, including Motorola, Nike, Boeing, General Motors, and

Hewlett-Packard. Four times a year it sends them a collection of new materials and gizmos with some very cool—and often amazing—properties.

For instance, the company has created electrically activated plastic muscles, which when zapped with electric stimulation can cause the material on a jacket or a running shoe to change its physical properties. For example, a shoe could grow more snug. Such a material would have obvious applications for a clothing or apparel manufacturer, but it could also trigger some creative juices for those in the medical device industry, who might see some applications for new health products.

Inventables has also created an absorbable silicon material. Better car bumpers for next-generation automobiles and flexible floors that help reduce the stress (and thus worker compensation claims) of workers who must stand long hours are just two possible applications.

Among the other items on the company's Web site are tiny sensors that can be used by cell phone manufacturers to create a phone that will sift through your e-mails with a tilt of your hand. There's also a spray-on material that can double as a chalkboard.

Another set of "toys" the exponential executive might consider employing are the new virtual-reality Web sites. Due to advances in graphics, computer processing power, and broadband capacity, 3-D immersive technology, while still crude, is no longer as futuristic as it once may have sounded.

The Web site Second Life has created an alternative universe where people can create avatars (computer animations of themselves). Adam Pasick, a reporter for Reuters, in 2006 became the first member of the media to begin covering the emerging world of virtual reality. He is doing so, of course, as an avatar.

Avatars can do everything from participate in company meetings (IBM now regularly holds such meetings online) to allow customers to browse through a virtual store and view products in three-dimensional form and then see how those various appliances might look in a room.

If your firm is considering doing business in Sweden, you might first visit the country's virtual embassy in Second Life.

One of the other benefits of virtual reality, in addition to saving companies real money by reducing travel budgets or providing better customer service, is that people, through their avatars, are able to take on different personality traits and personas. It might sound frivolous (and undoubtedly it can be), but it also offers businesses the opportunity to jump the curve by allowing people to step outside of their conventional roles. For instance, in Second Life an administrative assistant, whose ideas might ordinarily be dismissed because of his junior position, could pose as a manager and suggest an idea in an online forum, or, alternatively, an executive could disguise him or herself as a potential customer in order to experience firsthand how company employees service the client. In virtual reality, a person's age, gender, or job title means little. It also means that good ideas can come from anywhere.

Exponential INSIGHT

To help employees jump the curve and think about the future, it helps to give them the equivalent of a new toy pogo stick on occasion or allow them to spend a little time away from the office—even if it's only a virtual getaway. You never know what creative juices a new toy or a new venue might spark.

JUMP THE CURVE STRATEGY #17:
Think Visually

One of the benefits of being a child is that you are not yet wedded to particular ways of doing things. To demonstrate this point, let me give you a little quiz. Imagine that the following Roman-numeral equation is made out of ten sticks (for example, "X", "+" and "=" all represent two sticks):

$$XI + I = X$$

The goal of the exercise is to fashion the answer by moving around as few sticks as possible. How many sticks did you have to move to get the correct answer?

If you answered one (by turning the equation into the following: IX+I =X), you solved the problem, but that is not the correct answer. The correct answer is zero. Solving the equation requires that you merely flip the equation upside down. What is interesting about solving this problem is that when students had their brains scanned while solving the problem, researchers discovered that there was an abrupt decrease in the brain waves associated with both memory (delta waves) and conventional mental activity (gamma waves) immediately before people deduced the correct answer. This finding has led the researchers to theorize that thinking spatially might be one way to expand your problem-solving potential.

A case in point is Stephen Jacobson, the CEO of a company called Sarcos Research. His company, much like Inventables, is a skunk works for hire. It invents things.

Among Jacobson's many inventions is something known as the Utah Arm, a prosthetic arm that allows above-elbow amputees to control their elbow, hand, and wrist using only two muscles. Jacobson is also regarded as his company's most unconventional thinker, and when asked how he comes up with his ideas he has said that he visualizes projects. In his mind's eye, he will enlarge computer chips and tiny little sensors and spin them around to better understand where they might be best placed or how they might work with other components.

A related element of thinking visually is the importance of developing prototypes. How often have you gone to a meeting where a person is discussing an idea or a concept and the conversation stalls or meanders on toward no constructive ending in large part because there isn't an actual product to see, touch, or manipulate?

Contrast this with a meeting where someone has brought a prototype. How much more productive was the meeting? Moreover, who controlled the agenda? More than likely it was the person with the tangible item. David Kelley, the founder of Ideo, one of the world's leading design firms, likes to say, "If a picture is worth a thousand words, a prototype is worth a million words."

Exponential **INSIGHT**

In 1940 the U.S. Census Bureau eliminated the job category of inventor and relabeled it researcher. The difference is more than semantic. Inventors invent, while researchers investigate. One quick way to spur creativity and invention within a company or organization may be as simple as giving people a job title that more closely aligns with their responsibilities. To jump the curve, it helps if people are free to visualize the different places that a business can jump to.

JUMP THE CURVE STRATEGY #18:
Create Serendipity

Most people will agree that childhood can be an almost magical time. There are many reasons for this, but one of the least explored areas is the role serendipity—or making fortunate discoveries accidentally—plays in a child's youthful exuberance and upbeat attitude.

This attitude derives, in part, from the feeling that some new discovery or pleasure is lurking just around the corner or inside every box. Over time, the pleasure of serendipity is stripped from most of us because we no longer feel we have the time to indulge our inner curiosity. Either we think pursuing such things is frivolous or not productive or, alternatively, we convince ourselves that we have more pressing concerns that need to be addressed.

But when you think about it, what's more important than thinking about the future? As one wag said, "The future is where we are going to spend the rest of our lives so someone had better start thinking about it."

To jump-start the process, I recommend introducing some planned serendipity into your life. There are a number of ways to do this, but one of the easiest is to read a magazine or newspaper from back to the front. What this does is it cause the reader to reconsider the relative importance of every story.

Presumably newspaper editors have a reason for putting certain stories on the front page, but, really, who are they to tell the reader what's most important? Do they know technology? Do they understand scientific advances? Or perhaps they simply have a bias for political or human interest stories.

On November 16, 2006, as I was writing this section of the book, I decided to do this exercise with the front section of my hometown newspaper, the *Minneapolis Star Tribune.* I began by reading the editorial section. At the time, political pundits were still dissecting the recent midterm elections, and nothing much caught my attention. It continued this way until page A4 where I noticed a small one-paragraph story, no bigger than a typical obituary, noting that scientists in Texas had cloned a championship horse. A few years ago, such news would have been a page 1 story.

On the next page, A3, a second article informed me that scientists had unlocked the genetic code of our closest human ancestor, the Neanderthal. One researcher said she was "blown away" by the report, and another added that the findings "are perhaps the most significant contributions published in this field since the discovery of Neanderthals 150 years ago." The reason for this excitement is because it is believed that by comparing Neanderthal DNA against human DNA, scientists will be able to discern the few genes that distinguish you and me from Neanderthals, and this might help explain what makes us human.

On the same page there was another article noting—again without much fanfare—that researchers in Switzerland had coaxed stem cells into growing the first heart valve. It went on to quote a researcher in the field as saying that he "didn't doubt" this advance would one day be used to grow heart valve replacements for humans.

On page A2 an article reported that researchers at the University of Pittsburgh had injected stem cells to ease muscular dystrophy in dogs. It noted that an official at the Muscular Dystrophy

Association called the news "one of the most exciting developments" in years because it suggested that stem cells could also lead to advances in the treatment of muscular dystrophy for humans.

Finally I turned to the front page, and there was a large story documenting the enthusiasm being generated by Sony and Nintendo's new video games—the PS3 and Wii. It was an excitement that was vividly captured by the photo showing people camping out overnight in subfreezing temperatures in an effort to be first to purchase the new games.

As I read the article, I reflected on how it seemed only yesterday that my brother and I were tinkering around the start of the video game phenomenon as we battled one another in the game of Pong on our black-and-white television. I further reflected that as much as I liked Pong, it would have been impossible for me to imagine that in only three decades time the video-game industry would become larger than all of Hollywood (which it did in terms of revenue in 2005) and that colleges and graduate schools would be offering degrees in video-game design. Yet this is precisely what has come to pass.

The quote that really stood out for me in the article, though, was the one from the young video gamer who said, "It's amazing how much a part of our culture [gaming] is." It is amazing.

But because I had perused the paper backwards that day, I reflected on how so many modern medical advances have become an accepted part of culture. They are now regarded as inside news stories.

However, just as Pong and other video games have gotten progressively better and ultimately became a massive, multibillion industry that has now so infused its way into our culture that people are willing to wait overnight in the cold to buy the next-generation game system, by working a little planned serendipity into my day I came to better understand how stem cell research, DNA analysis, and cloning are also being infused in our culture. And I could more easily envision how pervasive these emerging technologies will become in the not-too-distant future.

Another path to planned serendipity can be found in the new media. One of my favorite Web sites is *www.digg.com.* The site is really nothing more than an amalgamation of news stories, articles, blogs, and videos that other people have found interesting enough to rank as being valuable or noteworthy for some reason.

What is fascinating about the site is that there is no editor. Instead the leading posts have risen to their respective positions on the basis of the collective actions of individuals from around the world. Those stories receiving the most votes, or "diggs," rise to the top of the site. The stories come from world of business, science, technology, politics, and the arts, and I can tell you I have come across an amazing amount of useful, informative, or just plain interesting information that otherwise would have escaped my attention.

Exponential INSIGHT

The future is fast approaching. It may not always be announced on the front page, but if you "digg" around and do things a little differently on occasion, you can sometimes catch a glimpse of the future and better discern where you and your organization might want to jump the curve.

JUMP THE CURVE STRATEGY #19:
Add a Little Sci-Fi to Your Reading Diet

Is science fiction the best predictor of the future? Not really, but when compared against the predictions of such magazines as *Popular Mechanics,* which famously predicted in 1949 that computers would weigh no more than 3,000 pounds in the future and electricity would be "too cheap to meter" (because of nuclear power), it doesn't look so bad. Take Jules Verne's Nautilus, the submarine in his 1870 novel *Twenty Thousand Leagues Under the Sea,* which popularized submarine technology more than a half century before it was widely adopted. Similarly William Gibson's 1984 novel *Neuromancer* envisioned aspects of the World Wide Web almost a decade before it reached popular culture, and Neal Stephenson's 1992 book *Snow Crash* anticipated by a number of years some of today's leading virtual-reality sites such as Second Life.

More recently still, researchers at the Robot Intelligence Lab in South Korea have developed a software robot that can easily transfer itself from computer to computer or even from a computer to robot. It is an innovative technology, but if a person read Frederic Pohl's 1965 novel *The Age of the Pussyfoot,* he or she might have wondered why it has taken so long to develop. In Pohl's book, every person had a device called a joymaker that allowed him to be in constant contact with the network. This intelligent agent even helped make decisions for a person because it was assumed there were so many options that a person could not reasonably be expected to know what the best option was without the use of the joymaker.

Think such a device is unlikely? Perhaps, but take a look at the software NetFlix and Amazon use to help customers determine which movie or book they might want to purchase, then jump the curve a little way and consider what might be next. If you are traveling to a new city and looking for a good restaurant, would you rather trust the local guidebook in your hotel room, or would you prefer to rely on a software agent that understands your personal preferences and tastes—right down to your penchant for Sri Lankan spicy food?

Exponential **INSIGHT**

Timothy Leary once said, "You're only as young as the last time you changed your mind." Science fiction offers the potential of changing your mind in ways that other books can't. To jump the curve it doesn't hurt on occasion to see where those people who are making their living by forecasting the future are heading. For as Isaac Asimov said, "It is change, continuing change, that is the dominant factor in society today. No sensible decision can be made any longer without taking into account not only the world as it is, but the world as it will be. . . . This, in turn, means that our statesmen, our businessmen, our everyman must take on a science fictional way of thinking." That especially includes the exponential executive.

JUMP THE CURVE STRATEGY #20:
Cut Down on the Ritalin

If you or your child is on Ritalin, I am not suggesting you take this advice of cutting down on the Ritalin literally. I'm not a doctor; this is only intended as a metaphor.

Within the medical community there is some debate over whether the widespread use of Ritalin is useful. While the drug is undoubtedly helpful in certain cases, opponents feel it may also be stifling some children's creativity. As a result, they feel too many "problem" children are shutting up and dropping out; young scientists aren't experimenting or concocting wild potions; and aspiring musicians, poets, and novelists aren't daydreaming new lyrics, figuring out new ways to touch our souls, or crafting the next storyline of the next science-fiction thriller that might offer a vista into the future.

As Jeffrey Zaslow wrote in the *Wall Street Journal,* "Kids on Ritalin are like horses with blinders on . . . they are more focused, moving forward and getting things done but they are less open to inspiration."

In many ways, the pressures and speed of modern society are forcing too many of us to put on blinders in the name of relentless increases in efficiency and productivity. This is obviously an important element of business success, but it can't be the sole focus.

CONCLUSION

The exponential economy is now moving so fast that disruptive change and paradigm shifts are becoming more the norm than the exception. Adjusting to this rapidly changing environment requires that we also learn to adapt, and one of the best ways to change is to exercise our brain and reestablish old neural connections or forge new ones that allow us to make fresh connections.

As I said earlier, play is a form of learning, and it helped all of us survive those treacherous years from birth to five when virtually everything was new to us. Now that the exponential economy is tilting the balance again toward new things, it will require us to return to our childhood roots and begin playing in the sandbox again. And just who we may want to play with in that sandbox of the future is the subject of our next chapter.

There is very little difference between one man and another; but what little there is, is very important. This distinction seems to me to go to the root of the matter.

—William James, *The Will to Believe*

CHAPTER 6

The Spice of Life: Diversity

It has been said that diversity is the spice of life. But diversity is more than just a spice, it is actually a necessary and vital ingredient of life. Consider a very close and intimate example: you.

Have you ever wondered how it is that you got to where you are? I am not speaking here of the mystery of life (although in keeping with the theme of the book I feel compelled to mention that the cell division that occurs almost from the moment you are conceived is but another example of exponential growth); rather, I am referring to your place in society.

That we even have a society to be members of is an enthralling proposition, and while I am sure a few people have pondered such a question in a moment of quiet reflection or perhaps in some long forgotten freshmen philosophy course, it is safe to say that most people have chosen not to make answering this question the central theme of their lives. Fewer still have decided to write a book about it.

To our good fortune, Jared Diamond did explore this very question in his Pulitzer Prize–winning book *Guns, Germs, and Steel.* The work seeks to answer the question of why different societies developed in different ways and progressed at different rates. Or as Diamond so eloquently phrases the question: Why is it that Africa, where protohumans evolved for the longest period of time, didn't come to develop the tools that would have permitted it to conquer Europe rather than vice versa?

As the book's title implies, the answer is not altogether simple. One of the principal and necessary ingredients behind Western civilizations' explosive growth from a small band of nomadic hunter and gatherers 10,000 years ago to today's hyperconnected, supersized international economy where billions of dollars pulsate electronically in the blink of an eye and hundreds of ships three times the size of a football field roam the high seas at any given moment is diversity.

More specifically, a diversity of weather, terrain, climate, plants, and animals lie at the heart of modern society's exponential advancement. As Diamond explains, it is not just a quirk of fate that civilization began in the Fertile Crescent. A confluence of diversity conspired to spark modern civilization. To begin with, the region was blessed with a wealth of altitudes and topographies. This gave rise to rivers, deserts, and flood plains, which, when combined with differing weather patterns in the region, produced a bewildering array of plants. In fact, ten millennia ago thirty-two of the world's fifty-six different wild grasses could be found in the Fertile Crescent.

These plants then cross-pollinated with one another and gave rise to an even wider assortment of plants. This potpourri of plants attracted an amazing collection of animals, including four species of big mammals—the goat, sheep, pig, and cow—that could be easily domesticated.

Ingenious hunter-gatherers who had already begun cultivating some of the perennial plants to supplement their hunting diet discerned a variety of uses for these animals. Not only did they use them for food and clothing, they also recognized that these beasts of burden could be put to work to provide traction and transportation for more difficult jobs, and they could be used to further exploit the land by providing fertilizer.

And it was this use of both plants and animals that gave humans their first big break because the abundance of calories and proteins that these crops and animals provided allowed even more hunter-gatherers to put down their weapons and forego their nomadic ways and instead, in confidence, pick up a hoe and begin farming.

Over time, increasing numbers of hunter-gatherers did the same, and soon there were enough people to require some organization. I am skipping a few steps here, but among the first things that needed to be done was that leaders had to emerge to delegate the tasks. Next bureaucrats were appointed to oversee operations, and soon after armies were created to protect the society's existing land as well as advance its search for more.

This combination of leaders, bureaucrats, soldiers, and farmers allowed for the creation of an even greater diversity of professions—civil engineers, builders, educators, scientists, financiers, medical specialists, and philosophers—to flourish over time. And these specialists begat more advances as each group contributed to the growing strength of the collective. The moral of the story is that while diversity does beget more diversity, the real advances—and the best way to jump the curve—is to figure out how to exploit that diversity.

JUMP THE CURVE STRATEGY #21:
Play Off Your Neighbor's Strength

Life on the African savanna can be a dangerous place, especially if you're an animal. Predators that possess astonishing strength, razor-sharp teeth and claws, and cunning camouflage lurk everywhere and are often just waiting to make some poor, less unfortunate creature on the food chain their next meal without the slightest compunction.

One strategy for surviving in this perilous environment is to be at least one step speedier than your slowest colleague. It is a fitting analogy for today's business environment and Juan Enriquez, in his book *As the Future Catches You*, summarized this line of thinking thusly: "Every morning a gazelle wakes and thinks, 'To stay alive, I have to run faster than the fastest lion.'"

It's a marvelous strategy provided you are fleet of foot. If not, the strategy is nothing more than a temporary salve for a day or two because as Enriquez adds, "Just over the hill, a lion has realized, 'I have to run faster than the slowest gazelle, or I'll go hungry.'"

Fortunately there is a better way of surviving on the African plains, and it offers two distinct advantages over this survival-of-the-fittest strategy. Moreover, it is instructive for businesses and organizations looking to remain competitive in tomorrow's exponential economy.

What is the strategy? Playing off your neighbors' strength. Many animals survive on the savanna by working in partnership with other animals. One of the better-known examples is the unusual affiliation among wildebeests, zebras, and ostriches.

Alone each species is vulnerable. Together, though, this unlikely triumvirate forms an impressive survival team. Wildebeests have very good hearing but poor eyesight and a distressingly poor sense of smell. Zebras, on the other hand, only have modest hearing but are blessed with very keen sniffers, while ostriches possess excellent eyesight. By relying on the relative strengths of the other animals, the trio can often detect predators well in advance and take the necessary precautions to keep the threat at bay.

The same tactic can be employed in today's business environment. The convergence of sensors and information technology within the health-care arena is causing leading medical providers to look to semiconductor companies as new partners.

On a different scale, some companies are even trying to form in-house teams that can do a better job of spotting potential dangers. For instance, Eli Lilly, the large drug manufacturer, now relies on groups of "semi-experts" to help it determine which drug candidates should be allowed to proceed to Phase III clinical trials. (The decision is not inconsequential because of the time, money, and resources at stake.)

To use the animal analogy, imagine marketing executives as having good hearing for helping determine which drugs will do best in the commercial marketplace, molecular biologists as having the best eyesight for determining which drug molecules might be most effective, and regulatory and legal specialists as having the better sense of smell in selecting the drugs FDA regulators might be willing to accept.

Of course, diversity isn't only useful in warning of lurking dangers; it is also helpful in avoiding traps in the first place. The classic example, which was so adroitly profiled in the classic book *Groupthink* by Irving Janis, is the Bay of Pigs fiasco—the Kennedy administration's ill-advised plan to send a group of Cuban exiles into a swampy bay in Cuba in the hopes of sparking a popular uprising against Fidel Castro's communist regime.

After the humiliating defeat, President Kennedy demanded his administration study the failure of the invasion. What he learned is that he and his staff—many of whom had been schooled at the country's top universities—were a cohesive group but they all tended to think too much alike. In short, his staff was not diverse enough.

Had Kennedy and his advisors sought the advice of other military experts, Cuban exiles, and other interested and knowledgeable parties outside of their immediate circle, the problem might have been avoided. (Luckily Kennedy learned his lesson and successfully applied many of the findings toward the peaceful resolution of the Cuban missile crisis just a year later.)

The business world is chock full of examples of businesses tapping into the power of diversity. Stephanie Capparell, in her book *The Real Pepsi Challenge*, documents how as early as the mid-1940s Pepsi had hired African Americans to figure out how to market Pepsi to "the Negro market," and as recently as 2004 the company determined that its continued commitment to diversity was responsible for attributing one full percentage point of its 7.4 percent revenue growth—or $250 million—to new products inspired by diversity.

Similarly Ford Motor Company credits one of its more notable successes of the past few decades to diversity. Many of the unique features of the minivan were not the work of clever and empathetic engineers but rather were the product of multiple minds working together to devise a product that would serve different people's needs. For instance, disabled workers recommended sliding doors, mothers looking for some help with storing their children's drinks asked for cup holders, and the elderly needed some assistance in discerning when obstacles might be behind them and requested a sensor that beeped.

Scores of other companies have also moved in a big way to embrace diversity. IBM, Google, and Microsoft among others are moving abroad and are doing so not only to be closer to their markets and have access to inexpensive and talented labor but also because Indians, Chinese, Europeans, and Africans all have different sets of "senses," and they can see, hear, or smell both threats and opportunities that are not always obvious to others.

Exponential INSIGHT

Like a predator waiting to attack, the next paradigm shift or disruptive technology is just around the corner. To survive these assaults, which will only become more frequent in the exponential economy, it is no longer enough to be the fittest. The key will be to surround yourself with people who possess different "senses."

JUMP THE CURVE STRATEGY #22:
Seek Six Degrees of Unity

Spotting new business opportunities is all about making connec-tions—connecting how a new advance in the material sciences can be applied to a new product, understanding how increases in capacity of data storage or bandwidth can create a new busi-ness model, or linking together how the convergence of advanc-ing technologies such as sensors, wireless Internet, and robotics could lead to a new product. For example, you might envision a home-security robot that could be controlled from your office and not only let the cable repairman into your house but watch over him until he completed the job and escort him out when he was done.

To help make such connections, it helps to have a diversity of people with unique skills and different talents. In some ways this can be considered to be a corollary to the six degrees of sepa-ration theory. This has been made famous by the Kevin Bacon game wherein people try to link the actor to any other film star via the movies they have starred in together. (To demonstrate I'll link Elvis Presley to Kevin Bacon using the example drawn from Wikipedia. Elvis Presley was in *Change of Habit* with Ed Asner, and Ed Asner was in *JFK* with Kevin Bacon. This gives Elvis Pres-ley a Bacon score of 2.)

One of the reasons Bacon is relatively easy to connect with other actors is because he has starred in a variety of movies— drama, action, humor, and so forth. In short, he is a diverse actor. On the other hand, an actor such as John Wayne, who starred in more movies but limited them to a narrow range (war and cow-boy movies) is more difficult to link.

The goal in the exponential economy is to become more like Kevin Bacon and less like John Wayne. You want to diversify your base of knowledge and expose yourself to a wider group of individuals who have an intellectual pedigree different than your own.

A simple mathematical equation illuminates the wisdom of this approach in generating new ideas. If you have just four people of different professional backgrounds, say an engineer, biologist, physicist, and chemist, it is possible to derive twenty-four unique combinations or pairs: $4 \times 3 \times 2 \times 1 = 24$. If, however, you add just two more individuals—say a computer scientist and a material scientist—the number skyrockets to 720: $6 \times 5 \times 4 \times 3 \times 2 \times 1 = 720$. Obviously the scenario is overly simplistic in that it doesn't account for the intellectual rigor of the different specialists, nor does it recognize that a good many people are able to think through problems from a variety of different perspectives. Nevertheless, the general point still stands: The greater diversity of people, the better the odds of spotting different opportunities, sparking new ideas, finding unique approaches to old problems, or creating innovative solutions.

To this end, it should be no surprise that in the past few years the number of people whom Nobel Prize winners have cited as having collaborated with them on their winning discoveries has increased immensely. The world is growing more complex, and even the brightest people are turning to others outside their areas of expertise for assistance.

The emphasis on different scientific backgrounds in the previous example may sound limited; after all, insights from marketing, legal, and business experts, or even artists, hold great value in the exponential economy. However, in today's society scientific knowledge lies at the heart of much of today's progress. It stands to reason, therefore, that one of the more productive methods for making connections and tapping into the potential of the exponential economy is to seek six degrees of unity among different scientific specialists.

A number of organizations in business, government, and academic circles are now doing exactly this. In late 2006 Google, the poster child of the innovative Web 2.0 culture, and NASA, an organization top-heavy with older engineers, agreed to work together on the convergence of nanotechnology, biology, information technology, and cognitive science (NBIC).

The benefit of this approach is that the two organizations each bring to the table individuals with a plethora of unique skills. The partnership blends the skills of young and old engineers, biologists, material scientists, physicists, chemists, engineers, computer scientists, and software engineers. It is hoped that by bringing together so many diverse people with different perspectives the two organizations will create newfound synergies.

The United States Army and MIT are doing the same at the Institute of Soldier Nanotechnologies. One of the more intriguing projects the group is working on is applying nanotechnology to create uniforms that can camouflage themselves instantaneously. To accomplish this chameleon-like stunt, the institute will draw upon the skills of molecular biologists, chemists, and polymer experts.

The benefits of six degrees of unity are not confined to giving our fighting forces uniforms that seem ripped from straight from Arnold Schwartzenegger's 1984 classic, *Predator*. Nike and Johnson & Johnson are both seeking to exploit the unique characteristics of the gravity-defying gecko to create better climbing shoes and an ouchless bandage. To do so they have hired molecular biologists to study and help re-create features of the gecko's adhesive feet.

Clothes that change color, shoes that don't slip, and ouchless bandages are not the sole benefits of six degrees of unity either. Ideo—the famous design firm whose founder is credited with creating Apple's first mouse and which has brought society such wonders as no-squeeze, stand-up toothpaste tubes—regularly employs psychologists, engineers, anthropologists, and even linguists to help companies design better products. Each specialty brings a unique perspective.

Cirque du Soleil is another example of this trend. One reason the troupe is able to keep its performances fresh, exciting, and innovative is because the company's management has created a transdisciplinary experience that mixes circus art, music, and stagecraft with artists from a multitude of cultures to produce performances that are not only visually stunning but singularly unique.

Exponential INSIGHT

The entrepreneurialism of Ideo and Cirque du Soleil is just a snapshot of the unique opportunities that await organizations bringing together people of different skills and backgrounds. To really jump the curve it is imperative to make even more connections. One way to do that is to tap into the open-source movement and broadcast your business-related problems to the outside world. The solutions that this most diverse of audiences will respond with is sure to astound you.

JUMP THE CURVE STRATEGY #23:
Listen to the Voices on the Fringe

Brilliant people, despite their genius, can have their faults. When I speak of faults in this context I am not referring simply to a genius's general indifference to those who are less clever or intelligent; instead, I am talking about an unwillingness to countenance theories that do not agree with his or her own view of the world.

An inability to consider other people's ideas or viewpoint is a dangerous handicap (especially in an era of exponential change), and it is not just a problem for smart people. It is also predicament that often afflicts the powerful—or those in positions of power.

In 2007, in a fascinating study, investigators asked people to draw an "E" on their forehead. The subjects were given no more information than that. Interestingly, people who were identified as powerful were three times as likely to draw the letter from *their* frame of reference—so that the "E" would appear backwards to others. The researchers theorized that this is an indication that powerful people have a harder time considering the perspective of others.

Personally, I believe there is something to the theory. The field of science is chock full of examples of brilliant scientists and even entire academic disciplines unable to consider new ideas. No less an authority than Lord Kelvin—who fancied himself the world's smartest man at the end of the nineteenth century—boldly declared in 1899 that "heavier than air flying machines are impossible." Luckily two obscure bicycle repairmen from Dayton, Ohio, saw fit not to listen, and the rest, as they say, is history.

In late 1970s, the general consensus among paleontologists was that dinosaurs became extinct over an extended period of time. Then in 1978, three scientists—a nuclear chemist, a physicist, and a geologist—advanced the radical notion that the dinosaurs' fate was sealed by a giant meteorite that struck the earth around 65 million years ago. They theorized that this catastrophic event spewed an other-worldly amount of dust and debris into the air and irrevocably altered the world's climate conditions in such a way that was not conducive to the dinosaurs' long-term survival.

The scientists were roundly mocked at the conference where they first introduced their theory, and later it was considered an "outrageous heresy." Three decades on with mounting evidence, while it is still a theory the "meteor theory" is no longer laughed at, and a great many paleontologists now accept it as fact.

An even more vivid example of the hubris of scientific experts can be found in Bill Bryson's book, *A Short History of Nearly Everything*, in which he documents the outlandishly absurd lengths the geology profession went to sustain their theory of how the fossils of the same species came to be found on different continents.

Rather than accept the possibility that the continents might have at one time been joined together in a single body of land (which, if you have ever looked at the west coast of Africa and the eastern coasts of North and South America and noted they look pieces of a puzzle doesn't seem that far-fetched), the geology community of yesteryear possessed enough mental elasticity to accept that a series of land bridges—in some cases 3,000 kilometers long—were a more plausible explanation for how various animals might have come to live on both continents rather than acknowledge the possibility that the continents might at one time have been part of a single body.

That is until 1944 when Arthur Holmes explained how the land masses could, over the course of millions of years, separate to great distances due to convection currents within the earth. Still, as late as 1963, a young Canadian geologist, Lawrence Morley, submitted his theory on continental drift to the *Journal of Geophysical Research* where it was promptly rejected by an editor with a snooty letter stating: "Such speculations make interesting talk at cocktail parties, but it is not the sort of thing that ought to be published under serious scientific aegis."

It is not my contention that every crackpot theory deserves to be elevated as fact. There are plenty of ideas that are not based in science and deserve to be roundly dismissed. But those who take the time to propose new ideas—and back it up with the rigor of science—should be heard.

A wonderful example is the case of Aubrey deGrey. In the February 2005 edition of MIT's *Technology Review*, deGrey had the audacity to propose that man could live forever, and he laid out a seven-step process for achieving this goal called *strategies for engineered negligible senescence* (SENS). To many scientists, researchers, and professionals in the medical establishment he was characterized as a crackpot and "a troll," and he was generally dismissed because he had a long, flowing beard, dressed like a shabby graduate student, and wasn't part of the establishment (he was the computer support to a research team at Cambridge University). Interestingly no one attacked his ideas directly.

One group of scientists even confidently declared that "a research program based around the SENS agenda . . . is so far from plausible that it commands no respect at all from within the scientific community."

A few months later *Technology Review* sponsored a contest to scientifically refute deGrey's theories. While it is important to note the judges did select a winner, the magazine offered the winning team only *half* the prize because their "careful scholarship" came closest to refuting his claims. In other words, deGrey wasn't proved wrong.

Ideas such as deGrey's, even if they are ultimately dismissed, deserve to be contemplated. Why? Because at a minimum they open people's minds to new ideas, new possibilities and, more important, they might cause some people to see old or intractable problems in new ways and to forge new solutions.

At a slightly more practical level, listening to the fringe can have other benefits. Susan Lyne, CEO of Martha Stewart Living Omnimedia, has said that TV hits "come from the fringe." As proof she cited *CSI*, the biggest hit of 2006, and noted that it was first turned down by a couple of networks before it was picked up. Even the decade's most popular show, *American Idol*, was turned down by every network, including Fox, before Rupert Murdoch agreed to listen to his younger daughter, who felt it would be a hit. His daughter was right; *American Idol* has become a phenomenal success.

Exponential **INSIGHT**

Marshall McCluhan once said, "I don't know who discovered water, but it wasn't a fish." The phrase perhaps best encapsulates this method of jumping the curve. So many new technologies are accelerating and converging in unexpected ways that it is unrealistic for any organization, however big, to think it has all the perspectives covered. If you want to minimize the prospects of being blind-sided by the next big thing, the exponential executive needs to lend his or her ear to those on the fringe.

JUMP THE CURVE STRATEGY #24:
Develop Decathletes

Since 9/11, few would argue that the world we live in hasn't changed significantly. The threats society faces are new, and the enemy is learning to adjust tactics in response to new technologies and is constantly innovating by using both new and old technologies in different and unexpected ways.

General Pete Schoomaker, the former Army chief of staff who left his position in 2007, recognized this early on and worked to change the U.S. Army during his tenure. To Schoomaker's mind, if the Army were a track team "it would have the best sprinters, the best milers, and the best discus thrower," but what it really needed to be doing was "making decathletes that are just good enough at everything."

In today's environment, where the pursuit of excellence and echoes of Jack Welch's claims to either be "number one or number two . . . or get out" are still lionized, the phrase "just good enough" has an unfamiliar and decidedly less edgy ring to it. But there is something to it. Rapidly changing conditions require leaders and organizations who can adjust with the circumstances, and in the future it may very well be that it is better to be good at four or five different things than great at just one.

A few years back, business leadership guru Warren Bennis wondered aloud how it was that more than two centuries ago America, with a population of only 3 million, could produce no less than six leaders of extraordinary and historic stature. He included in this august group George Washington, John Adams, Thomas Jefferson, Benjamin Franklin, Alexander Hamilton, and James Madison. He then further wondered how the country today, with a population of 300 million, couldn't even seem to come up with two leaders of similar stature to run for president.

Not the least reason for this is that many individuals of immense talent chose not to put themselves and their family through the grinder that has today become known as modern politics—but there is another reason. Few people today have the breadth and diversity of knowledge that that distinguished group possessed. Our forefathers were knowledgeable in military warcraft, diplomacy, business, economics, history, philosophy, agriculture, biology, and the natural sciences. In short, they were Renaissance men.

This diversity had many side benefits. It enhanced their curiosity and likely humbled them when they contemplated the many things they still didn't know. This duality likely played a role in Thomas Jefferson's controversial decision in 1801 to make the Louisiana Purchase and send Meriwether Lewis and William Clark west to explore this new acquisition.

To better prepare Meriwether Lewis, Jefferson demanded that he first go to Philadelphia to bone up on everything from natural sciences and medicine to celestial navigation. To say that at the completion of this crash course Lewis was an expert in any of those fields would be to stretch the truth, but it is fair to say that he was good enough. He was a well-trained decathlete.

Exponential INSIGHT

Although the Journey of Discovery is most closely associated with Lewis and Clark, it is safe to say that both men understood that even their combined skills weren't good enough to guarantee success in conquering the unknown environment they were about to explore. To compensate for their shortcomings they embraced diversity and chose men from all parts of the country. They looked to the Appalachian region for men who had experience with climbing mountains as well as to river states, such as Tennessee, for those who were knowledgeable about and comfortable around the water. In essence, they sought to achieve six degrees of unity.

Lewis and Clark even hired from the fringe. They selected no fewer than six men of Native American descent because they knew these men's unique perspectives (and language skills) were likely to come in handy. When push came to shove during critical junctures of the journey, the two leaders were even open enough to using the skills and talents of Sacagawea, the young Indian teenager, and William Clark's black slave, York.

To further bolster the enterprise's prospects of success, Lewis played to his remaining weaknesses and selected William Clark to be his coleader. At the time, it was an extraordinary decision because the military thrives on a strict adherence to a chain of command—it likes to have a single person be in charge. And yet Lewis was smart enough to recognize that he could benefit from a man who possessed different skills than he. Put another way, if Lewis had to draw an "E" on his forehead, he probably would have written it such that it could read by others.

CONCLUSION

The Corps of Discovery successfully navigated 5,000 miles of unchartered territory and battled everything from raging rivers, ferocious grizzly bears, frigid winters, and massive mountains. In the process, they also set America on a new westward course, and their success would not have been possible without embracing diversity—not for reasons of political correctness but for the sake of successfully navigating the unknown.

The same is true today. To be sure, the forces that will make tomorrow's environment unknowable will be more technological in nature (not to mention less physically dangerous) than those the Corps of Discovery encountered, but they will be no less daunting. To survive and prosper, it will be necessary to embrace the principle of diversity. The idea of seeking out different individuals with different skill sets and hiring people with different perspectives or who live out on the fringe might seem a little counterintuitive to building a cohesive team capable of jumping the curve, but as we will see in the next chapter, it is just the beginning of thinking in a counterintuitive manner.

Study the art of science and the
science of art.

—Leonardo da Vinci

CHAPTER 7

Heads and Tails: It's Counterintuitive

Quantum mechanics. The very term conjures up images of intimidating mathematical formulations, memories of perplexing theories, and, if you were like me, poor grades in high-school physics class. Today, if the topic somehow works its way into our daily conversation, it is enough to send most of us scurrying for the nearest exit.

Fortunately the topic isn't discussed much, which, if you really think about it, is kind of surprising considering that fully one-third of the global economy is now based on the exploitation of principles elucidated in quantum physics. Transistors, the heart and soul of the semiconductor industry and the basis for much of Silicon Valley, rely on quantum physics as do lasers, light-emitting diodes, fiber optics, and an assortment of other products which are now household staples.

What makes all of this so amazing is that for all of its practicality, quantum mechanics is still only partially understood. For example, we know that at the quantum level materials can be both gaseous and solid; currents can flow clockwise and counter-clockwise simultaneously; electrons can function as both a wave and a particle, spin and stand still at the same time; and, astonishingly, can be both here and there at the same time.

As Bill Bryson wrote in his breathtaking and absorbing book, *A Short History of Nearly Everything*, electrons move between orbits and disappear from one and reappear in another without visiting any space in between. "This," Bryson notes, "is rather like a person being under surveillance showing up in a specific location without ever being seen traveling between locations."

To put it mildly, at the quantum scale the rules for understanding the world around us begin to break down. It is rather unsettling then to think that so much of our economy and way of life hinges on the exploitation of principles that are only partially understood.

This reliance, however, will only continue to grow more prominent in the future. Steve Waite, in his book *Quantum Investing*, estimates that by 2025 well over half of the global economy will be based on the exploitation of quantum physics. To compound any unease you might feel at this prospect, he further conjectures that it is not unreasonable to believe that by that time at least twenty-seven of the thirty companies currently comprising the Dow Jones Industrial Average might no longer be part of the index—victims of new companies that have figured out how to better harness the unique features of quantum mechanics and translate them into new commercial products.

How is one to survive in an environment that relies on principles that even the great genius Einstein called "spooky"? One trick is to borrow a trait from quantum mechanics and learn to embrace the counterintuitive notion that something can be two different things at the same time. To use an example from everyday life, imagine a world where a coin flip no longer automatically results in an outcome of either heads or tails. Instead a third outcome now exists, and that is that the coin can be both heads and tails at the same time.

As F. Scott Fitzgerald wrote over eighty years ago, "The test of a first rate mind is the ability to hold two diametrically opposed ideas in your head at the same time." The exponential economy will call upon this skill in spades. Fortunately the trick is not nearly as complicated as learning or understanding quantum physics. In fact, we need only recall a lesson from grade-school mathematics to grasp the basic idea. The equation 2x=4 has two different answers: 2 or −2. Specifically, $2 \times 2 = 4$ and $(-2) \times (-2) = 4$.

In its simplest form, if you can grasp the logic behind this equation, you are on the path to using counterintuitive thinking to jump the curve.

JUMP THE CURVE STRATEGY #25:
To Speed Up, Slow Down

The entire premise of this book is that today's economy is moving so fast that it requires people to think radically different than they have in the past. Therefore, it might surprise you to learn that one counterintuitive method of jumping the curve—or in this case it might be more appropriate to call it a quantum leap— is to purposely slow things down.

In December 2006, researchers at IBM announced that they had figured out a way to slow down the speed of light. Never mind for the moment that they only figured out how to do it for a half of one nanosecond—or one-half of one-billionth of a second. This advance was heralded as a major milestone because it strongly suggested that within the next decade researchers will be able to manipulate light to construct computer chips significantly faster than anything on the market today. In other words, slowing light will mean faster communications. It is a perfect example of slowing something down to speed it up.

A slightly more practical method of envisioning this trait is one of life's pesky problems: the all-too-frequent traffic jam. How many times have you shifted over to a faster moving lane only to be slowed down moments later and watch in frustration as the slower lane from which you just escaped moves along at a brisker pace?

One of the reasons this occurs is because the faster a car is moving, the harder the brakes must be applied when it needs to stop. This in turn causes the car following to slam on its brakes even harder. James Surowiecki refers to this as a "wave of deceleration." Therefore, counterintuitively, if everyone went a little slower, everyone would go faster in the long run because there would be less braking.

More to the point, as businesses and executives alike move into the exponential economy, a variety of tools are being developed to keep businesses moving by preventing them from having to hit the brakes as often. Two specific examples are computer modeling and rapid prototype design. By playing out specific scenarios on computers or constructing model designs in advance, businesses can avoid the equivalent of "waves of deceleration."

New and improved software tools are also playing a similar role. IBM and others are now developing sophisticated software that can enhance people's productivity by keeping them from a variety of work habits that are not that productive. Many people, for example, check their e-mail or BlackBerries far more frequently than is productive. New software programs are now on the market (with more on the way) that will sift through employee's e-mails, calendars, schedules, and even their work documents to better understand their priorities and alert them when an item requires their attention.

One last example further illustrates how slowing something down can work to one's advantage. Years ago, one of the major complaints surrounding elevators was that people hated waiting for them to arrive. Engineers tried to address the issue by making them go faster, and although they were slightly successful, people quickly adjusted to faster car times and just raised their expectations.

As the complaints grew at one particular hotel, a manager asked his employees for possible solutions. Stymied, one person flipped the problem around and asked an odd and counterintuitive question: How could the hotel make people want to wait longer for the elevator?

One answer to this question was mirrors. By installing mirrors, it was reasoned, the hotel might persuade people to spend more time at the elevator looking at their appearance and adjusting their clothing or hair. Therein was the solution to the problem. When the hotel gave people something else to do—namely look at themselves—the number of complaints dropped.

Exponential **INSIGHT**

As the world moves ever faster, it is natural to want to move just as fast. But sometimes, if you take a moment to slow down and reflect on things, a new model will come along that will keep you moving faster or, as in the case of the mirror, keep your customers at bay. To this end, in 2007 researchers demonstrated that many of those business meetings you and your colleagues are constantly racing to attend may actually be making you dumber. In certain cases, people have a more difficult time coming up with new and alternative solutions when they are part of a group. The researchers speculate that the more one option is discussed the harder it is to recall other options and identify new ones. So, if you ever needed an additional reason not to attend your next office meeting, now you have one.

JUMP THE CURVE STRATEGY #26:
Stand Your Problems on Their Heads

It has been said that "necessity is the mother of invention." In fact, the refrain is so common that it is now accepted as conventional wisdom: If you want to create a successful business find a problem and solve it. As Jared Diamond explains in *Guns, Germs, and Steel*, however, this isn't necessarily so. In fact, a compelling argument can be made that just the opposite is true.

To bolster his counterintuitive claim that "invention is the mother of necessity," Diamond writes that "many or most inventions were driven by curiosity or by a love of tinkering, in the absence of any initial demand for the product they had in mind." Included in the list of products falling into this category are the airplane, automobile, light bulb, transistor, and phonograph. As further evidence he cites no less an authority than Thomas Edison who, when he first published a list of the things for which the phonograph might be used, failed to mention reproducing music as one of those possibilities.

All of this is to say that a second method of thinking counterintuitively is to stand both products and problems on their head. To this end, one area of today's business economy undergoing radical transformation is the often overlooked field of material science. In the haste of daily life it is easy to forget how much materials have improved our lives—everything from our thermally insulated coffee mug to the comfy Gore-Tex jacket that wicks away sweat during our daily jogs.

The importance of material science isn't going to change; if anything, it's going to speed up. Nanotechnology, the field of manipulating atoms and molecules, has been called the ultimate in material science. Large companies such as GE and BASF as well as dozens of smaller ones such as Aspen Aerogels are pouring millions of dollars into the field and will continue to do so in an effort to create materials that keep coffee piping hot for longer periods of time and more efficiently and discreetly dispose of runners' sweat.

The exponential economy, though, is an era of unheralded imagination, and to fully exploit its potential businesses need to think differently. So different, in fact, that it might help to begin looking for opportunities at the opposite end of the business spectrum.

Using the coffee thermos as an example, what if it were possible to create a thermos that not only kept coffee warm but actually made it hotter? With advances in thin-film photovoltaics, such a device might soon be possible.

Similarly, using Gore-Tex as an example, what benefit could be derived by making a person sweat more? If there were a way to harness the body heat of the person and convert it into electricity, it would be possible, among other things, to create solar fabrics to act as a supplementary power source to help recharge a cell phone, iPod, or a laptop computer.

If the idea sounds silly, just consider this: The average weight of the equipment a soldier now carries into battle varies between 90 and 120 pounds—or roughly the equivalent of what the average Roman legionary carried over 2,000 years ago. Much of this weight is from the heavy batteries soldiers need to power many of their electronic communication devices.

Thermal-electric clothing or solar fabrics—clothing that harnesses photons from the sun and converts them into electricity—could lessen the burden of these batteries for not just real warriors but road warriors as well. Walk through the airport and count the number of electrical devices the average business traveler is carrying, and a sliver of the opportunity that such materials might create becomes apparent.

A number of companies are already employing advances in material science to stand existing problems on their heads. Pilkington and Asahi Glass have created new windows that get cleaner—not dirtier—when it rains. This nifty little trick is pulled off by embedding nanoparticles of titanium dioxide into the glass. These particles react with the photons from the sun to break up dirt and other pesky contaminants, which are then flushed away by the next rain.

Nike offers another useful example of standing a problem on its head. Consider the Free Shoe, which aims to mimic the sensation of running barefoot. First, its name aside, the shoe is nowhere near free. It retails for about $89. Second, a shoe that mimics running barefoot is indeed standing a problem on its head. Although humans have gone to a lot of trouble of cover their feet over the years, da Vinci correctly observed that the human foot "is a masterpiece of engineering and a work of art" and doesn't really need any assistance. After all, bare feet served our ancestors just fine for thousands of years.

Progress in a number of fields is now advancing so rapidly that standing problems on their heads is just one way to stay ahead of the curve. A few years ago I stumbled across an article that explained how a tobacco executive, Bennett LeBow, was trying to help people quit smoking. The method LeBow proposed was to get them to smoke *more*.

As a result of advances in genetic agriculture, LeBow learned that researchers had devised a way to grow tobacco with nary a trace of nicotine. It was LeBow's contention that since nicotine is a major contributor to most people's addiction to tobacco, if his company could grow a tobacco leaf with varying levels of nicotine, he could slowly wean smokers off tobacco by offering them a line of cigarettes that had progressively less nicotine. To my knowledge, the product hasn't been a major success in part because the rest of the tobacco industry has not looked kindly on the project—but it does represent a fine example of standing a problem on its head and using technology to approach an old problem in a new way.

The exponential economy will offer many other such opportunities. Can people lose weight by eating more? As our understanding of genetics increases, it is possible. Similarly, can traffic congestion be reduced by having people drive more? The answer is a qualified yes to the extent that sensor technology could help individuals take a slightly longer route home but one which doesn't entail as many waves of deceleration. Can children learn more by playing more video games? Again the answer is yes. In the summer of 2006, the *New York Times* published a fascinating article that demonstrated how students and adults had a much better understanding of the Israel-Palestine conflict after playing a video game because it required them to assume the role of one of the parties. By experiencing how every action they undertook elicited a response by their opponents, the players came away with a deeper appreciation of the realities of the conflict as well as a better understanding of the motives and plight of the other side.

Exponential INSIGHT

Henry David Thoreau once said that people gain a new perspective on their world by looking at it from a different angle. One quick way to look for inspiration or gain an unexpected insight is to view a problem upside down. The small town of Hidalgo, Texas, did just this when word spread a few decades back that its location placed it smack dab in the middle of the migration path of African killer bees. Rather than engage in a slick public relations campaign to minimize the issue or assuage people's concerns, city officials boldly proclaimed the town "killer bee capital of the world" and constructed a massive replica of the dreaded insect. The decision has been a boon to tourism.

JUMP THE CURVE STRATEGY #27:
To Move Forward, Step Back

A few summers back all of the local news channels in my home-town led their evening news with the tragic story of a young man being attacked by a shark off the coast of North Carolina. What made the story so curious was that I live in Minnesota, and the nearest ocean is more than a thousand miles away. I suppose it is mathematically possible that a rogue genetically mutant shark might somehow miraculously navigate the St. Lawrence Seaway and survive in the cool waters of Lake Superior long enough to stage an attack on some unfortunate soul for whom surfing the modest, albeit frigid, waves of the North Shore is a pleasurable activity. But I think most people would agree that devoting min-utes of airtime to such a remote possibility is silly—especially when so many other real threats are lurking out there.

It being a sweeps month, the TV executives were most likely motivated less by educating viewers of the nonexistent threat of shark attacks in Lake Superior and more by attracting their attention with sensational news, but the absurdity of it all was brought into refreshing clarity the next day when a professor of statistics revealed that the average person is twenty-seven times more likely to perish as a result of a television falling on her head than of being killed by a shark.

Unfortunately this mildly comforting nugget of information was buried deep within a section of a local paper next to the obituary section where, if it was read at all, it was likely noted by people old enough to appreciate that on the list of things to worry about being consumed by shark should not be anywhere near the top.

It was not without some irony then that just six months later I stumbled upon another sad story in the newspaper about a young child in Minnesota dying after being crushed by a falling television. The story received no television coverage and barely warranted a second paragraph in a small story on page B7 in the local section of the newspaper.

The dichotomy of the time and attention devoted to the two separate events highlights one of the key tenets of Steven Levitt's and Stephen Dubner's best-selling book, *Freakonomics,* that people tend to *overreact* to events where the hazard of the event is low but the sense of dread or outrage is high (a shark attack) and *underreact* when the hazard is relatively high but the outrage is low (a falling television).

Levitt and Dubner use the example of the disproportionate response of people to the accidental death of a child by a gun found in a person's home as compared to the reaction when a child drowns in a neighbor's pool. The vast majority of the publics' and politicians' attention is focused on the former, even though an accidental death by drowning is fifty times as likely to occur.

The point of these findings is that world is awash in data and if one steps back for a moment and reflects on the data, surprising things can be found—findings that are, well, counterintuitive.

Let's consider for a moment the story of Abraham Wald. As a young man during World War II, the Hungarian-born mathematician served as a statistician and undertook a study on behalf of the British Air Ministry. Among his responsibilities was to assess the vulnerability of Allied airplanes to enemy fire. The intent of those who commissioned the study was to devise methods to better protect the aircraft.

Therefore, as the airplanes returned from their sorties, they were diligently assessed for damage. It was soon apparent from all the existing data that certain parts of the plane—such as the tail—were being damaged disproportionally more than other parts of the plane.

Naturally this led RAF officials to recommend that those areas of the plane be reinforced with extra armor. Wald, however, reached just the opposite conclusion. He argued that data was only being collected from the planes that successfully completed their mission. It didn't include those unlucky enough to be shot down in battle.

Recognizing that this created a selection bias, Wald came to the counterintuitive conclusion that the parts of the returning planes that were *not* riddled with holes should be the areas that receive additional fortification. Why? Because he understood that those areas of the aircraft that had been hit and yet still made it back were not critical to the mission's success.

The advent of RFIDs, sensors, memory spots, and inexpensive computer chips that can wirelessly transmit reams of information will only add to the growing heaps of data in coming years. The opportunity to distill hidden nuggets of information from this data is immense.

The trick for the exponential executive is to be receptive to what the data suggests, because some of the findings will appear counterintuitive. For example, in 2006, Tesco, the large British retailer, began offering beer coupons to first-time buyers of diapers. What the company's data sleuths uncovered was not that British women, who had foregone months of drinking during their pregnancy, were suddenly intent on making up for lost time and quaffing a few brews; rather, they found that many first-time fathers—men who could no longer go out to the pub with their friends on the weekend because of their new paternal responsibilities—still enjoyed an occasional beer and were amenable to picking some up malt beverages whenever they had to go to the store to buy diapers. By discovering the connection, Tesco was able to increase sales of diapers and beer, as well as its profits.

The opposite of not discerning patterns is seeing patterns where none exist, and this can be as just costly as not spotting connections. From the time we are infants, humans are able to recognize patterns, and over time we become so good that, as one wag has said, we often see pattern where none exists.

Wall Street financiers looking for trends, a parole board assessing a criminal's prospects for recidivism, and weathermen are just a few of the many professionals who look for patterns. Even doctors, who are trained to recognize patterns in faint coughs, mysterious red blotches, and vaguely described ailments, have been known to subscribe medications for a problem that doesn't exist.

This is not to condemn doctors, weathermen, or parole boards when they make poor predictions. All are doing their best, often under very difficult circumstances, and more often than not they have access to a limited amount of information. Instead I want to highlight that there is still a stunning amount of room for improvement in most businesses' basic decision-making processes and that exponential advances in technology can be employed to help address this shortcoming.

Let's consider medical doctors. They're required to spend seven years of their lives in intense study and several years following medical school gaining practical experience before they earn the right to treat patients. But advances in biotechnology, nanotechnology, proteinomics, and scores of other fields are occurring so rapidly that even if a doctor devoted herself full time to reading periodicals and attending conferences, she still couldn't possibly keep up on all the new medical information. Therefore it is unrealistic to assume that doctors will always be able to make the correct diagnosis or recommend the appropriate course of action.

Technology can help. According to a 2006 study in the *British Medical Journal,* doctors were able to correctly diagnose rare diseases in 58 percent of the cases simply by typing the ailments as keywords into Google. This percentage will only increase in the future as advances in health-related information, data storage, algorithms, and wireless and broadband communications all converge to increase doctors' ability to diagnose disease even better. The trick will be to stay open to the idea that a computer might discern patterns that run counter to conventional wisdom.

Exponential **INSIGHT**

From falling televisions and neighbors' swimming pools to bullet holes in the tailfin of a plane and rare diseases, what you don't know could literally kill you. To jump the curve, sometimes it helps to step back before leaping forward.

JUMP THE CURVE STRATEGY #28:
Less Is More

It is a little-known secret that many of today's most successful companies, such as General Electric and IBM, are betting big money that one of the larger future trends will be the continued growth of megacities—or cities that have a population of 10 million or greater. In 1950 only two megacities, New York and London, existed. By 1985 the number had jumped to nine. Today there are an estimated twenty-five.

With more than half of the world's 6 billion people living in these and other densely populated urban areas, it makes sense for businesses to focus on developing products and technologies that address these populations' unique needs. To deal with many of the associated urban problems, one of the more popular strategies urban planners have adopted can be labeled "smart growth." The term has different meanings, but the essence of it can be summed up as doing more with less. Ideas include packing more people into the same amount of space, pricing roads to accommodate a greater number of automobiles, and producing less pollution per person.

Jumping the curve requires thinking long and hard about how exponential advances might help achieve these goals. Doing more with less is yet another way of doing this. The earlier example of the robotic system that allows sixty-seven cars to be parked in a space that used to fit only twenty-four is a case in point. Another example is using new nanomaterials to reduce the smog in populated urban areas. One British company, Oxonica, is now producing a nanoparticle-enhanced fuel additive, which when added to diesel not only increases the mileage that can be obtained from the fuel, but also reduces the smog-producing emissions.

Many other emerging technologies are decreasing the cost of products once deemed to be the purview of the higher echelons of society. Take the automobile for example. In 2007 Toyota announced that it would employ a number of new technologies in order to produce a new line of automobiles for $6,000.

It is a good idea because it is really a less-is-more twofer. To begin with, advances in computer technology enable cars to be enhanced with more features at a lower price, and new nanomaterials are helping Toyota construct the car with less material.

The second good feature of the idea is espoused in C.K. Prahalad's book, *The Fortune at the Bottom of the Pyramid*, which postulates that because only a fraction of the world's population actually constitutes the higher tier, there is a vast amount of money ($13 trillion) to be made by targeting products at the middle and lower end of the economic pyramid. The exponential executive must consider how other technologies, such as voice recognition and increased bandwidth, might open up additional business opportunities to serve customers at the bottom of the pyramid.

For example, Hewlett-Packard developed technologies to enable low-cost digital picture taking and printing. Dubbed the HP Photoshop Store, the technology is now sold throughout India. The company has even developed an accompanying camera that is powered by a solar backpack.

Another spin on this less-is-more tactic can be found in the broad outlines of Chris Anderson's book, *The Long Tail*. The premise of the book is that the old 80/20 rule—80 percent of one's business is derived from 20 percent of one's customers or 20 percent of one's products—no longer applies because of businesses' and consumers' ability to easily store and transmit vast amounts of information in a digital format.

For instance, it had previously been accepted that only the best-selling books, movies, and records generate a profit for the producers of those products. The remaining items simply occupy shelf space in stores.

As more and more products become digitized, the cost of storing that inventory and distributing those products has fallen so dramatically that the economics of those lesser-selling products has also changed. According to Anderson, Rhapsody, a music downloading service, now makes as much money from selling songs beyond its top 10,000 list as it does from its best-selling 10,000 songs. Similarly NetFlix generates one-fifth of its sales from movies that aren't even ranked in the top 3,000.

Just fifteen years ago less than 1 in 800 people had access to the Internet. That meant that capturing a sliver of that market—say 0.1 percent—was a still relatively small number. Today over 1 billion people have access to the Internet. If a Web site or product can reach just one-tenth of 1 percent, that is 1 million people. Many businesses can survive by finding and serving such meganiches.

Consider one example: candy. According to the book *Candy-freak*, a century ago there were more than 6,000 different candy manufacturers in America but today there are only a handful. Do markets still exist for obscure or different candies? Absolutely. The Internet now offers the exponential executive an opportunity and a method to find, aggregate, and serve those audiences of people who love Idaho Spuds, GooGoo Clusters, Abba-Zabbas, Twin Bings, Necco Wafers, and, my personal favorite, Clark Bars.

Exponential **INSIGHT**

Nassim Taleb, in his captivating book *The Black Swan,* offers a wonderful example of this idea of less is more, and it is related to many executives' insatiable need for more information—more reports, more data analysis, more newspapers, and so on. In the book, Taleb writes, "Additional knowledge of the minutiae of daily business can be useless, even actually toxic." To demonstrate he cites the example of two groups of people being given a blurry image of a fire hydrant. One group had the resolution of the photo increased ten times, the second only five times. Counterintuitively, the group that was given less information was more likely to recognize the picture for what it was because they formulated fewer hypotheses along the way.

JUMP THE CURVE STRATEGY #29:
Turn into the Crash

Growing up in Minnesota where winter is a six-month endurance sport, one of the life skills residents learned before the era of antilock brakes was how to control an automobile in snowy and icy conditions. One of the more difficult tasks to master was how to bring your hulky automobile to heel in the event it began to skid dangerously out of control as a result of an encounter with a hidden patch of black ice.

The trick, as one was taught at the tender age of fifteen, was to point the steering wheel into the turn. This is all well and good provided that all you need to do was respond with that answer on a written test to obtain your driving permit. It is altogether something different to employ the skill under the duress of an actual emergency (such as skidding toward a snowy ditch) because of its counterintuitive nature.

I mention this because as exponential advances in technology continue to propel society down the freeway of the future at accelerating speeds and as yet-to-be developed technological advances sprout up, they may create the equivalent of hitting a spot of black ice. And keeping a company or organization on the road will require leaders, at times, to engage in practices that seem as counterintuitive as pointing the steering wheel into the direction that a person wishes to avoid.

Exponential INSIGHT

In 2006 Nintendo shocked the video-gaming world by introducing its new video-game console, the Wii. Unlike Sony's supercharged PS3 or Microsoft's Xbox, Wii didn't have fancy graphics and the console wasn't even targeted toward avid gamers. Rather it relied on a sophisticated network of sensors to help people mimic activities like bowling, tennis, and sword fighting. It was so easy to use that even nongamers flocked to it. There are now even Wii bowling leagues for the over-sixty-five set.

By targeting nonconsumers with something less complex Nintendo was able to beat the big boys at their own game, and so can you. All you need to do is turn into the crash on occasion.

Clayton Christensen, in his two best-selling books *An Innovator's Dilemma* and *An Innovator's Solution*, makes much the same point by advising companies to do two things: One, don't always listen to the needs of your best customers, and two, focus on those folks who *aren't* your customers.

Both tactics are counterintuitive, but they are essential to dealing with disruptive technologies. And if anything is going to be a staple of the exponential economy, it will be the accelerating development of disruptive technologies.

CONCLUSION

If you think that thinking counterintuitively is, well, counterintuitive, consider this: Who would have imagined five years ago that a group of people working for free could produce an encyclopedia that is on par with the *Encyclopedia Britannica*? Or who, just ten years ago, would have imagined that people would have so much data storage on their music devices that they would pay a company (in this case Apple) to provide them with a method for randomly shuffling their music so they don't have to do it themselves, or that seniors would represent the fastest growing market segment for video-game manufacturers?

Thinking differently and holding opposed ideas in your head at all times will be an essential skill set for prospering in the exponential economy. So too will the notion of embracing both the concepts of nurture and nature as determinates of future success. In fact, the next chapter focuses on how organizations can nuture nature to the benefit of organizational growth.

Study nature, love nature, stay close to nature. It will never fail you.

—Frank Lloyd Wright

CHAPTER 8

Get in Touch with Your Animal Instincts

The great inventor and artist Leonardo da Vinci was fond of urging both artists and scientists to go straight to nature when in search of inspiration. If you have ever seen a picture of the conch shell-shaped spiral staircase at the castle in Blois, France, which da Vinci designed, you know that he practiced what he preached.

It is unknown if George de Mestral, a young Swiss engineer, was familiar with da Vinci's advice when he went for a stroll with his dog in the summer of 1948, but he seems to have taken the message to heart. When the pair returned from their walk they were covered with cockleburs—those wretched plant seed sacs that cling to almost anything (usually animal fur) in the hopes of catching a free ride to more fertile planting ground.

After defrocking himself and his dog, de Mestral's curiosity was piqued, and he took a few of the burrs to his microscope to review what made them cling so tenaciously to his pants. He was amazed to find that each burr consisted of hundreds of tiny hooks that could grab on to loops of thread or animal fur.

He immediately recognized the value of this unique fastener and understood that it offered a viable alternative to the much used—and venerated—zipper. Unfortunately this insight was not instantly recognized by others in the fashion industry.

De Mestral was not to be deterred. With the help of some fabric and clothing experts in France, he worked to mimic the burrs and soon discovered that nylon when sewn under infrared light could fashion a light hook that was sturdy enough to match the characteristics of the burr. In 1955 de Mestral patented the technology, which he called Velcro—as in a combination of velour and crochet. Today it is a multimillion-dollar business.

Finding inspiration from Mother Nature is hardly new. From da Vinci's designs to paint companies that have mimicked the extraordinary water-repelling and unique dirt-cleansing properties of the lotus to more recent attempts by companies to reverse engineer the gravity-defying properties of the gecko's feet, people have intuitively understood that there is a lot to learn from the world around us.

Consider the humble newt, which has learned how to regrow limbs, and the rather ordinary zebra fish, which possesses the quite extraordinary ability to regrow its own heart. Given that millions of Americans are believed to be at risk of some form of heart disease, the ability to mimic the *Brachydanio rerio* (the scientific name of the zebra fish) could be the basis of a multibillion-dollar industry.

Closer to home, one company that has already taken this lesson in biology to heart is Daimler. Following an exhaustive search of the natural world in search of inspiration to help design its next-generation automobile, the company's researchers passed over sleeker and sexier candidates such as sharks and dolphins and instead found inspiration in the *Ostracion meleagris*, or the spotted boxfish.

On the face of it this choice might seem odd because the box-fish, looks, well, like a box and boxes are not typically appreciated for their mastery of aerodynamics. A closer examination of the boxfish, though, reveals the fish's pronounced wedge shape, prominent descending rear, and heavily scalloped sides all combine to produce an almost ideal drag coefficient of .04. As an added benefit, the boxfish also has a surprisingly low bone mass that has been perfected by evolution to be stronger in areas where the fish can expect to receive more stress and less dense in those areas that are not subjected to as much pressure. In short, the boxfish is a model of aerodynamic efficiency, and it has achieved maximum strength with a minimum use of material.

By mimicking all of these properties, Daimler expects to design more fuel-efficient vehicles that are both lighter and more aerodynamic. Initially it was felt that consumers wouldn't pay for something as visually unappealing as a car shaped after a boxfish, but given the success of Honda's superspacious albeit boxy SUV, the Element, it is possible that a boxfish-inspired car will make it to the commercial marketplace.

Even if it doesn't, Daimler engineers have learned many other things that will make their way into its future automobiles. For instance, parts of the cars subjected to lower loads will be made thinner and lighter but in a way that doesn't compromise passenger safety, and outside mirrors (which increase the drag) will be replaced by inside cameras that do a better job of providing drivers a picture of what is going on to the side and behind the vehicle (no blind spots). By more closely aligning the properties of the car with the laws of nature—as exemplified by the boxfish—Daimler believes it will be able to create an automobile that achieves somewhere between seventy and eight-four miles per gallon.

According to Janine Benyus, author of *Biomimickry*, this is just the tip of the iceberg of what is possible to learn from Mother Nature. Biological knowledge, like so many other things, is doubling every few years, and scientists and researchers are now just beginning to comprehend the astonishing things Mother Nature has concocted over the past 4 billion years in her vast and wonderful research and development lab.

What the exponential executive will need to do is make like a flea—which can leap heights sixty-five times greater than its own height—and get ready to jump the curve by tapping into the vast wealth of biological knowledge that exists in the natural world.

JUMP THE CURVE STRATEGY #30:
Follow the Ants

To begin our quick jaunt across the biological world in search of help in dealing with the complexity of today's accelerating technological advances, let's begin with that most humble of creatures— the ant. Lest you think this is an odd place to start, I feel compelled to mention that no less an authority than the Bible provides this same advice when it advises its readers in Proverbs 6:6, "Go to the ant thou sluggard; consider her ways, and be wise."

Without reflecting on the more philosophical nature of the quote and wishing to remain ecumenical in outlook, I will confine my remarks to ants' uncanny ability to collectively find new and productive food sources even though no one single ant knows where the food is. Ants have devised a simple method of solving the problem. As they wander to and fro searching for food they deposit small traces of pheromones. When an ant locates some food it retraces its path back to the other ants, and the pheromone scent becomes slightly stronger because it now has twice the level of pheromones. This attracts the attention of other ants, which follow the same path. In so doing, the scent becomes even stronger and the track is reinforced with ever more pheromones. In essence, the ants use this information to locate food sources and build paths that optimize their use of time and energy.

This method of optimization—sometimes called ant hill optimization—has been employed by FedEx, which has devised comparable methods of leaving trails of digital information to optimize its routing and transportation systems. France Telecom has used similar techniques to more efficiently route information between communication nodes. The principles can also be used for supply-chain management, factory scheduling, and even controlling groups of robots.

To a degree, the same process is at work with Google's search engines and other popular Web sites. In Google's case, Web sites that are frequented more by other users will have a stronger scent, if you will, and *www.Digg.com* and other such ranking

Web sites use individual voting preferences to act as electronic pheromones.

The more people who "digg" a story, the more likely it will rise to a prominent place on the Web site where it may receive additional reinforcement. The exponential executive can jump the curve by using similar tools to get an early indication of what is and what isn't hot.

Interestingly, ants also possess a method for ensuring that new food sources are constantly being identified. It is sometimes referred to as a wild hare or the pioneer ant method, because often an individual ant will break off from the group in search of a new food source. As Michael Mauboussin explains in *More Than You Know*, it is the equivalent of a fail-safe mechanism that allows the ant community to exploit existing food sources while ensuring that future opportunities are constantly being identified.

In many ways, the pioneer ant is a useful metaphor for making sure that a company or organization has at least a few individuals whose job it is to stay alert for new trends and search out new ideas. It also reinforces the idea outlined in Chapter 6 of the importance of hiring from the fringe. This is because such rogue individuals are most likely to stray from the beaten track and pick up scents of new emerging opportunities first.

> ### Exponential **INSIGHT**
>
> In nature, solutions to problems are emergent rather than preordained. As Eric Bonabeau, a leading scholar on swarm intelligence, has said, "Today, many managers would rather live with a problem that they can't solve than live with a solution they don't fully understand or control." In the exponential economy, managers will need to let go and sometimes just follow the ants.

JUMP THE CURVE STRATEGY #31:
Crawl Like a Bug

It will likely not surprise you that the Defense Advance Research Projects Agency, the Defense Department's cutting edge research lab that has brought society such wonders as Arnet (the precursor to the Internet), GPS, and stealth technology, has also tried to create mechanical elephants and weaponize bees. The agency has also commissioned projects such as Wolfpack (designed to create a pack of miniaturized sensors that could jam enemy communications), Piranha (aimed at helping submarines engage in elusive maneuvering), and Hummingbird Warrior (an unmanned aerial vehicle that can take off and land vertically). DARPA has even experimented with implanting neural chips into the brains of sharks and dolphins to control their movement for the purpose of using them as spies or possibly even to deliver explosives to enemy combatants.

Suffice it to say, DARPA has a rich history of looking to the animal kingdom and/or exploiting animals in the name of national defense. But such initiatives are just the beginning of DARPA's efforts to explore the natural world. Among the biological creatures the agency is studying for inspiration are snakes, spiders, termites, and even cockroaches.

For instance, pit vipers are known to have exquisitely sensitive tongues that can "smell" the air for other animals. DARPA is exploring how to transform this capability into a new tool for Navy SEAL divers that gives them a new way of receiving information. As it stands right now, the Navy's warriors are inundated with audio and visual information that they receive through a variety of communications devices.

By mimicking the sensing capability of a snake's tongue, Navy SEALs could receive information via an infrared tongue. As far-fetched as the idea seems, it could help alert soldiers to certain dangers. For instance, a tongue sensor could create a sour sensation to tell them if something was behind them. If the matter was of greater urgency, perhaps the sensor could even unleash a more bitter or burning sensation.

Does this tool have any practical implications for business? That's difficult to say, but if one considers where video-gaming and virtual-reality technology are headed, is it that much of a stretch to imagine that some innovative video game designers might try to incorporate a similar technology into the next generation of video games? (Perhaps something along the lines of a Pavlovian response, gamers could be rewarded with a pleasurable taste for reaching the next level of difficulty in a game.)

Another insect that has generated much enthusiasm and attention is the spider, whose silk is up to five times as strong as steel. Unlike steel, however, silk is manufactured at room temperature and with no expensive materials and no waste.

If researchers can mimic the creation of silk, it is believed they could create plastics that are lighter, stronger, and more environmentally friendly than anything on the market today. The U.S Treasury might also produce counterfeitproof bills that don't tear, the automobile industry could create fenders and airbags that better absorb the energy from a collision's impact (this is because spider silk is quite elastic), the marine industry could use it to manufacture stronger and thinner ropes and nets, and the medical industry might find such a material useful for producing better sutures or as a replacement for artificial ligaments and tendons.

Where is all of this material to come from, you ask? Well, back in 2000 a company bred goats to produce silk protein in their milk. And while that project hasn't exactly panned out, given the exponential advances in gene sequencing and researchers' better understanding of biology, it is entirely possible to think that a similar process might replace it in the near future.

Termites and beetles are two other creatures that have recently come to the attention of enterprising businesses. For instance, the African termite has demonstrated that it is capable of designing large mounds that are so well ventilated that it can keep its occupants cool at a constant temperatures even during those stretches of African afternoon when temperatures reach 100 degrees and higher. The termites' model has now been pilfered by architects in Africa who have constructed a skyscraper in Zimbabwe based largely on its design. As one engineer said, "If termites can maintain an acceptable, uniform environment, why not humans?" Indeed.

In a separate effort, researchers at MIT are studying the Namibian desert beetle to better understand how it collects water from fog. It is hoped that the material on the beetles' wings can be replicated to create devices that allow homes and businesses in water-depleted areas to more effectively capture the water that exists in the early morning mist. Such a material would have a wide variety of uses in those parts of the world where clean water is scarce or fresh water needs to be better conserved.

Still other beetles are also being investigated for their keen infrared sensing ability. The jewel beetle, for instance, is capable of detecting a wave of heat from up to twenty-five miles away. If scientists can determine how the beetle does this, it could lead to a highly sophisticated sensor that would have military, industrial, and even household applications.

Other researchers are exploring how cockroaches are able to climb walls. Companies are interested in applying the cockroaches' unique skills to manufacture robots that can climb walls to clean windows. The military, on the other hand, is interested in learning how the cockroach adjusts and adapts after it loses a limb. This is because in battle situations (or first-responder situations such as police and fire departments are likely to encounter), if something goes wrong and a robot is damaged the researchers want a robot that is able to carry on with its mission in spite of losing an appendage.

All of this leads us back to DARPA, which is so impressed with the many opportunities that Mother Nature represents for robots that it has created the Biologically Inspired Multifunctional Dynamic Robots Programs, which goes by the unwieldy and user-unfriendly name of Biodynotics.

Exponential **INSIGHT**

Today's business environment can be likened to a jungle, and in the future it will only become more hazardous. To survive it may be necessary to make nice with some insects. Who knows—a spider may help weave you a new safety net, a jewel beetle may alert you to an opportunity on the distant horizon, or a cockroach may help you adjust if a new technology has rendered one of your products irrelevant.

JUMP THE CURVE STRATEGY #32:
Take a Short Safari

If crawling things leave you a little creeped out, perhaps a jungle safari will be more to your liking. If so, you're still in luck because there is some inspiration to be found there as well, and it goes beyond the example of diversity that the wildebeest, zebra, and ostrich provided in Chapter 6.

Take, for an example, an elephant's trunk. In spite of its size it is a remarkably versatile instrument. It can scoop up a tiny peanut just as easily as it can move a heavy tree trunk. It is an ability that, if it could be transferred to a robot, would have great utility in helping soldiers and other firefighters use the robot to quickly remove heavy debris and possibly even usher injured people to safety.

Another notable animal is the rhinoceros. Its horns are a potent weapon; less well known is that the horns can repair themselves. This is all the more remarkable because the horn is made out of the same material that sits on your head: hair. This means there are no living cells in the material. Somehow, though, the material around the crack disassembles and flows back into the crevice where it is promptly reassembled into an instrument worthy of charging a Land Rover.

If a rhino can do this with its horn, is it possible that material scientists can construct a new-age glass, wood, plastic, or even concrete that could self-repair itself? Time will tell, but just imagine if an automobile's paint could repair scratches, and cracked bridges or roads could repair themselves. Among other things, insurance claims adjustors and highway repairman could become the equivalent of this century's chimney sweep because their jobs may no longer be needed.

Exponential INSIGHT

Not everything we can learn from the jungles of Africa relates to such functional things. Consider the baboon. It has been found that the difference between male baboons who live a long life and those who live a short one often depends on the ability of the older baboons to recruit younger ones to protect them. To return to the theme of diversity covered in Chapter 6, perhaps a young biologist or anthropologist can help your business survive longer in the jungle of today's business environment by opening your eyes to new ways of doing business.

JUMP THE CURVE STRATEGY #33:
Look to the Skies

Still stuck for inspiration? Turn your eyes to the sky. Any number of flying creatures can also provide insights for organizations looking for creative solutions to vexing problems. Consider the humble bumblebee. A number of writers have explored the waggle dance that bees do to alert other members of their hive to the merits of a potential new home.

The enthusiasm with which an individual bee waggles is used by the other bees in the hive to select among the various choices that other scout bees present them. The bee that waggles the most is believed to be the most enthusiastic about its site. This reaction helps the others in group select the best location even though most of them have never been to the site.

Any number of new systems are being employed today that pick up on this theme. In the fall of 2006, the online investment newsletter *The Motley Fool* (to which I am a regular contributor) unveiled its CAPS system. The system, in its simplest form, allows an individual investor to rank thousands of stocks according to whether the individual believes they will outperform or trail the market over different periods of time. The accuracy of the investor's predictions are then ranked.

In one sense the system allows investors to tap into the wisdom of crowds by seeing how many other people have ranked a certain stock. On a higher level though, not all recommendations are accorded equal weight. The higher a person's overall accuracy, the more weight his or her vote is given. In short, everyone can waggle, but the system is rigged to allow people to see who the best wagglers are and which stocks those wagglers are pointing others to.

Amazon.com, NetFlix, Digg.com, and others are also perfecting this art by allowing everyone to make comments about books, movies, and news stories but also allowing others to rank or comment on the usefulness of those recommendations. They are all creating systems that allow other people to find useful information faster.

In addition to bees, larger flying creatures have their merits as well. Hummingbirds are being investigated for their many unique characteristics, among which are their ability to stop in midair, turn on a dime, and even fly backwards. All are properties that are of no small interest to the military, which is busily developing small, flying robotic devices that can fly down alleyways and chase, photograph, and, if necessary, terminate with extreme prejudice enemy combatants. The military's thinking is simple: Why should it send $100 million jet fighters after insurgents when a relatively inexpensive hummingbird-like UAV might be able to do the job instead.

The flexible skin of bat wings is yet another biological wonder that is being investigated for both its ability to help the bat maneuver in tight spaces as well as its role in generating lift and reducing drag.

On a still larger scale are eagles, which have been found to possess an unusually high concentration of light-sensitive cells in the center of their eyes. This trait allows them to continue to focus on small distant objects without losing sight of what is happening on the periphery. The ability to mimic this skill would have applications for flying drones as well as security cameras, which might need to focus in on some suspicious movement on the distant horizon without compromising its ability to remain concentrated on the broader picture.

An elegant algorithm the business community might learn from birds is how simple rules of engagement can allow complex organizations to operate with great efficiency. Next time you are at the airport and are waiting to board your plane, take note of how plane after plane is lined up on the runway and each must await an order from the air traffic controller before being allowed to take off. Contrast this strict command-and-control system with the simplicity of how a huge flock of birds can take off with nary a bump.

Why is this? It's because birds follow three simple rules: 1) they always head toward the center of their neighbor, 2) they match the speed of their neighbor, and 3) they avoid collisions. With the advent of supersmart onboard computers and ultrasensitive sensors, modern aviation should be able to mimick these rules. And if they do, just imagine planes taking off not when some faceless bureaucrat in a landing tower says it is okay but rather as soon as the last passenger has boarded the plane.

Unrealistic? Perhaps, but if birds can do it, maybe humans will be able to do it some day as well.

Exponential **INSIGHT**

The earlier example of how an eagle can focus on the distant horizon without losing sight of the bigger picture is a good analogy for the exponential executive to consider. Threats that can appear to be off in the distant future are often closer than they might appear. Recall that in the exponential economy each new doubling matches all the progress of the previous advances—combined. In such an environment, things have a way of catching a lot of people off guard, and to survive people will need to adjust their vision to accommodate today's rapidly changing environment.

JUMP THE CURVE STRATEGY #34:
Go Fishing

Seeing as how almost three-fourths of the earth is covered by water, it makes sense that the oceans and its many occupants offer a wealth of bioinspiration. The humble sponge, for instance, is a master of self-assembly and is able to produce superfine glass fibers using nothing but seawater. It is a trick that many optical communication companies, which rely on glass fiber to transmit reams of data, would be very interested in learning to replicate. Other companies are exploring the idea of generating energy via massive underwater mills that are powered by the shifting tides. One problem is that the systems do not react well to extreme conditions. Kelp, the large seaweed, also generates its energy from the movement of the ocean, but its method of dealing with violent weather is to lie flat—which, researchers now believe, might also be the solution for the underwater mills.

The abalone offers yet another captivating example. The giant marine snail is easy to dismiss, but a few researchers have been captivated by its beautiful mother-of-pearl interior. Besides this richly colored nacre, the outer shell is even more noteworthy because its material is twice as tough as the best ceramic material known to mankind today, and it is created at room temperature. The best manmade ceramic material, on the other hand, must still be heated in a kiln up to 4,200 degrees Fahrenheit.

Some material scientists believe that if they can replicate the abalone's superhard, easy-to-manufacture material, a variety of real-world products including pipes, tiles, jet engine turbines, and biomedical implants might be given enhanced properties and could be manufactured in a less expensive yet more environmentally sustainable manner.

One researcher, Angela Belcher, has taken the abalone's fine example of self-assembly one step further and is actively exploring how the technique might be used to grow batteries and even semiconductor components. The idea might sound a little strange, but Belcher's rationale is quite solid. Think of it this way: Today the semiconductor industry is making incredibly small components—transistors in the range of fifty nanometers (or about 100 times smaller than a cell in your body)—and it is doing this through an unbelievably complex process that requires bouncing light off of nanoscopic mirrors to etch away silicon. And it is doing these things in fabrication facilities that cost billions of dollars and need to be upgraded or built anew every few years.

Needless to say, it is a cumbersome and costly proposition. Belcher and others are now asking the question: Why go to all this trouble when Mother Nature has demonstrated that individual atoms and molecules can be snapped together like Lego blocks at room temperature using little more than a glass beaker to mix the appropriate atoms together?

Still another sea creature that has come under the scrutiny of researchers is the multifaceted and fascinating octopus. With its powerful tentacles and astounding ability to morph its body shape and even camouflage itself, scientists see no shortage of real-world applications that this mollusk could inspire. For example, the octopus has a translucent reflecting protein that reflects all wavelengths of light. This allows the octopus to conceal itself whether it is shimmering along the bottom or drifting near the top of the ocean against a mixture of blue and white light. One possible application is a stealthlike material for the military.

If you combine all three characteristics of the octopus—its powerful tentacles, its ability to change shapes, and its skill in camouflaging itself—the amalgamation not only produces a powerful underwater weapon, but it could also create a robot that could help oil companies lay and repair sea piping in deep and difficult-to-reach areas. Such a robot could even help scientists research and find new types of heretofore unidentified or unknown sea creatures with yet-unknown amazing properties that are waiting to be discovered by us landlubbers.

Exponential **INSIGHT**

In early 2007, Craig Venter, the man largely responsible for mapping the human genome, undertook an expedition of the world's oceans. He and a crew of scientists took samples of microbes all along the way.

Interestingly, the expedition managed to triple the number of proteins known to science, and these proteins have potential applications in everything from the production of energy to the creation of new pharmaceutical products. Most of the proteins were found in the microbes floating on the surface of the oceans.

If one further considers that, when measured by weight, microbes are the most important part of biology on this planet, Venter's trip suggests that mankind has only begun to scratch the surface of what we might be able to learn from biology.

JUMP THE CURVE STRATEGY #35:
Seeking Bioinspiration

In the movie *Master and Commander*, there is a wonderful scene in which Captain Jack Aubrey, played by Russell Crowe, has seen his ship badly disabled in a previous battle and knows he is about to be attacked again. As he ponders his crew's and his ship's survival, he spots a walking stick bug and marvels at its ability to camouflage itself and use its disguise to capture its prey.

Captain Aubrey draws upon that inspiration and orders that his crew make it appear as though their ship is just a whaling vessel. The ruse works, and when the enemy draws near to investigate, the British unleash a surprise attack that wins the day. To my knowledge, the scene isn't based on a real example from naval history, but it offers a useful metaphor for thinking of Mother Nature as a source of inspiration.

Another way to think of Mother Nature is that she is a very resourceful, successful, and long-lasting business—one in which the animals, fish, birds, and other organisms can be thought of as products. If you follow the analogy you will note that all the bad or unsuccessful products have been recalled by evolution over the past couple of hundred million years. Those that have survived are the products of relentless evolution and have learned to operate in a highly efficient and successful manner that does not waste time, energy, or natural resources. This evolutionary success has much to teach business leaders about doing things differently and, often, in a more energy-efficient and sustainable manner.

CONCLUSION

Janine Benyus has said, "The definition of success in the natural world is keeping yourself alive and keeping your offspring alive 10,000 generations from now, and that's a tough thing to do." She's absolutely right. Living in today's exponential economy is difficult too, and it is tough enough to survive the next generation—let alone 10,000—but one good way to do it is to look to the biological world for ideas and inspiration.

Who knows? You might stumble upon a promising trail like an ant, repair your business with the flexibility of a rhino horn, remove obstacles with the dexterity of an elephant's trunk, find a new niche deep in some undiscovered market with the flexibility of an octopus, or even take a lesson from history to find out how it was that dinosaurs were able to successfully rule over the animal kingdom for some 165 million years. This last notion of using history to better prepare us for the future is the subject of the next chapter.

The farther one looks back, the farther one can see ahead.

—Winston Churchill

For prophecy based on an extension of the known has substance.

—Vannevar Bush

CHAPTER 9

Back to the Future

In the January 1, 2007, edition of the Proceedings of the National Academy of Sciences, an article appeared entitled "Neural substrates of envisioning the future." The gist of the article was that for the first time neuroscientists—using functional MRI—had identified the regions of the brain involved in envisioning the future. What they found is that the parts of the brain used when trying to envision the future are the same parts of the brain that are used to recollect the past. This suggested to the researchers that "to effectively generate a plausible image of the future, subjects reactivate images" of the past. Or, as another publication put it, "To imagine the future, we remember the past and put our projection in that context."

This notion lends some credence to that old quote, often attributed to Patrick Henry, who said: "I know of no other way to judge the future but by the past." Being an amateur historian, I have personally found that history is a wonderful way of illuminating the future. However, as the theme of this book might suggest, the process of using history to think about the future cannot be a linear one.

To explain why, let's consider human life expectancy. Today the average life span is approaching eighty years. This is an extraordinary leap from a century ago when life expectancy was forty-seven years and more than a doubling from the sixteenth century when Thomas Hobbes so famously depicted life as "nasty, brutish, and short." He was right. When he lived, life expectancy was only thirty-seven years.

Longer life expectancies, in combination with the accelerating pace of technological change, are now presenting society with an opportunity that wasn't available to our ancestors: People now *expect* to experience dramatic change in their lifetimes.

This wasn't always the case. For instance, 300 years ago the lives of our ancestors from one generation to the next were essentially the same. More often than not, a person lived and died in the same place as his parents and worked at the same jobs with the same tools as did his parents and grandparents.

In the past 100 years this situation has changed radically. It was not uncommon for many of our grandparents to have lived through the widespread introduction of electricity, the automobile, the airplane, antibiotics, and into the early stages of the information revolution.

As sweeping as these changes were, however, our grandparents did have some historical perspective to guide them. In some ways, the previous century's development of railroads portended the rapid movement of peoples and goods. The creation of the first synthetic drugs promised advances in new medicines, and the invention of steam power sparked the possibility that new sources of energy—such as electricity—might be exploited as well.

We ourselves are living in the midst of the information revolution, and it is safe to say that most of us would have shrugged our shoulders if we were asked only five years ago to identify the terms *blog, iPod, wiki, VoIP,* and *Web 2.0.* But we at least have some historical framework for this level of change because we have been subjected to the Internet, cell phones, and the personal computer—all devices that would have been unfamiliar just thirty years ago.

How, though, does one prepare for the radical acceleration of technology? In his illuminating book, *The Singularity Is Near: When Humans Transcend Biology,* Ray Kurzweil suggests that the accelerating pace of change means, among other things, that the amount of progress citizens will experience in the twenty-first century will be the equivalent of 20,000 years of progress using the "old" twentieth-century rate of change. That's right, 20,000 years. Even if Kurzweil is wrong by a factor of ten that would still mean that society would experience the equivalent of 2,000 years of progress this century.

One example will demonstrate why things are picking up speed so quickly. In March 2006 I wrote an article for a publication explaining that IBM was working with Rensselaer Polytechnic Institute to develop a supercomputer capable of 70 trillion calculations per seconds—a seventyfold increase from 1996 when Intel boldly announced that a computer using its chips had broke the 1 trillion calculations per second barrier.

As a method of explaining what 70 trillion calculations was, I wrote that if a person wanted to conduct the same number of calculations using a hand-held calculator, it would take that person approximately 60 million years to do what that supercomputer could do in one second—assuming the person was superhuman and could work twenty-four hours a day, 365 days a year.

Alas, IBM and others weren't satisfied with 70 trillion calculations per second. Just six months later, in October 2006, the company announced it would be producing a supercomputer with a capacity of a mind numbing 1 quadrillion calculations per second. Then, as if this weren't enough, in December it revealed its researchers were quite confident that the company would be able to produce a supercomputer capable of 10 quadrillion calculations per second by 2010. (For those counting at home, it would now take you eight billion years to do what this supercomputer will soon be able to do in one second. You might be relieved to know, however, that the sun itself is set to expire in five billion years, so you would be freed from this drudgery before you could finish the task.)

While many of these early supercomputers are being devoted to important but relatively mundane tasks such as trying to predict weather conditions or understanding the complex dynamics of thermonuclear explosions, some scientists are turning supercomputers' attention to fields that may yield startling breakthroughs. I have spoken earlier about advances in gene sequencing, protein folding, and the development of better materials, but one of the things these supercomputers will also be able to do is turn their focus inward—on themselves. That is to say that one of the first tasks these powerful supercomputers will do is go to work constructing a more potent successor.

What has been created here is called an *autocatalytic process*—a situation whereby one technological advance facilitates the creation and development of a next-generation tool, which then does the same for the following generation and so on. This continues in a virtuous cycle (or perhaps vicious cycle depending on your perspective) that grows ever swifter and more forceful as it progresses.

My point with this little example is to merely demonstrate that if we want to envision where society might be headed in 10, 25, or 100 years, we cannot afford to look back a comparable period of time and extrapolate forward. To understand where we might be in ten years, we need to look back at the past twenty-five years of progress. To comprehend what the world might be like in twenty-five years, we must consider the past 100 years. And a century hence, we need to look back between 2,000 and 20,000 years. Such are the dynamics of exponential growth, and it helps explain why to jump the curve effectively the exponential executive will sometimes need to leap far back in history to gain a proper perspective on what is coming.

JUMP THE CURVE STRATEGY #36:
Stretch Your Historical Imagination

As I explained back in Chapter 6, diversity played an integral role in getting all of us to where we are today. But, as is so often the case, there is more to the story. Technology itself has also played a key role in our progression through time, and every so often a variety of forces converge in such a way as to propel all human-kind down the path of progress at an accelerated clip.

Often these spurts of advancement are the product of an autocatalytic process. For example, roughly 13,000 years ago food production became the initial catalyst for one such phenomenon. As Jared Diamond explains in *Guns, Germs, and Steel*, what happened after the first food-producing society became successful is that the task of child rearing became much simplified because families—primarily women—no longer had to cart around their young children around as the men hunted for food. This freedom to stay in one location allowed women to more easily have more children and thus raise larger families.

With more mouths to feed, more food needed to be produced. This facilitated the invention of new techniques and technologies to produce, collect, process, harvest, and store food. This success facilitated an even more rapid transition away from hunting and gathering.

A similar transition took place about 500 years ago with the invention of the printing press. As Diamond explains in his book, the invention of the printing press—much like the agrarian society—did not simply materialize out of nowhere. A confluence of products, tools, and materials united at that specific moment in human history to foster the creation of the printing press. Paper, movable type, metallurgy, presses, inks, and scripts all had to be created before Johann Gutenberg could create his masterpiece.

Once they were there for the taking, Gutenberg put them all together and another autocatalytic process was born—the advancement of knowledge. Taking the form of books, information and knowledge began spreading rapidly and in unexpected ways, and this dissemination resulted in the creation of even more knowledge.

The same thing is again happening today. I've already talked about the example of the supercomputer, but just imagine the further spread of knowledge as computers become faster, smaller, cheaper, and better; as the Internet grows more powerful; as virtual reality becomes more immersive due to haptic technology;

and as advances in biology, genomics, and the neurosciences allow us to better understand the human body and the human mind.

Add to these innovations advancements in nanotechnology, software design, and rapid prototype design, and suddenly it becomes possible to envision a future whereby virtually any physical object can be printed. All that is required is software programs which can model the precise molecular makeup of a product and a printer-like device which can translate that code into a precise molecularly model of the object.

The consequences of engaging in such long-range speculation can, however, be perilous, as the following example shows. In 1730, in an attempt to get ahead of the curve in terms of the amount of knowledge that the printing press was creating, Trinity College in Dublin announced it was going to build a library to house all of the books that would ever be written. The proprietors of this ambitious undertaking estimated that this number would be 120,000. (How they arrived at this number is unknown.)

In less than a century, progress had overtaken them and there were already more than 200,000 books. Officials needed to enlarge the library and added a new roof. It still wasn't enough. Today there are approximately 100,000 books published annually and the number is growing thanks to the creation of the personal computer, the Internet, and publishing software. It is now possible for anyone to create her own masterpiece and with a click of a button send it to one of the many companies specializing in self-publishing and receive back in a matter of days a hardbound, colorful tome.

It is easy to laugh at the attempts of Trinity College to build a library to house every book ever written. But what is really funny is not that they built the library too small but, as history has now demonstrated, they built it too big.

How so, you say? Well, in 2007 Seagate, Hitachi, and other computer memory manufacturers began selling and marketing hard drives (about the size of a large book) capable of storing 1 terabyte of information—or the equivalent of 30,000 books. Today it is estimated that the Library of Congress possesses over 130 million catalogued items, including 29 million books.

This implies that it would require only 967 1-terabyte hard drives to store the equivalent of all of the books now occupying shelf space at the Library of Congress. Put another way, if those hard drives were located inside the library at Trinity College, they would (once digitally configured and stored) occupy less than a floor of the library. As an added benefit, the storage technology costs only a fraction of what it cost to build the original library three centuries ago.

Exponential INSIGHT

Before an autocatalytic process takes root, the new world it will create is scarcely imaginable. No more could Johann Gutenberg foresee that in 500 years the average person would have access to 29 million books than we today can envision what the world will look like fifty years out. Stretching one's historical imagination can be helpful in envisioning the future. It opens the mind to the amazing possibilities that await us and may even make the exponential executive more receptive to those possibilities when they do appear on the horizon.

JUMP THE CURVE STRATEGY #37:
Don't Laugh

In the fall of 2006 I attended MIT's annual conference on emerging technologies. One of the highlights was a presentation by Sebastian Thurn, the Stanford professor who was the head of the robotics team that captured DARPA's $2 million prize for building the first robot to successfully navigated a 132-mile course without any human intervention. As part of his presentation, Thurn showed various video clips of a robotic motorcycle manufactured by Stanford's crosstown rivals at the University of California at Berkeley. One clip showed the robot sputtering off the start line and crashing a few feet later. The next clip documented Cal-Berkeley's robot a year later as it staggered out of control after about fifty yards and barreled into a haystack. And the third and final video showed Cal's robot clearing the haystack before veering off at a dangerous angle into a ditch of water. Each clip was met with laughs from the audience—including myself.

The more I thought about those clips, the more I thought about those early black-and-white movie films one sometimes sees on the History Channel of early aviation pioneers in white lab coats, leather caps, and goggles who have strapped themselves in rickety, wooden biplanes that they then pathetically crash moments later.

From a distance of 100-plus years, the grainy films make the men look clumsy and silly, and it is easy to think of them as being a few cards short of a full deck. But that isn't the case at all. Many of the people in those films were among the brightest scientists and researchers of their generation, and they had dedicated a considerable amount of time, energy, and money in pursuit of creating the future. That their attempts failed is understandable. That their setbacks are now ingrained in our historical memory as ignominious failures is unfair.

The same is true with the robotic motorcycle. Sure, the technology didn't work in any of its early demonstrations, but if one observed closely there was something else going on. At first the robot didn't even make it off the starting line. In the second clip it did, but it was wobbly. In the third the wobble had been corrected, but it was only able to steer in a straight line for the length of a football field. If one stops laughing one thing is patently evident: substantial progress is being made each year.

It is too early too tell how progress will be made in 2008, but it is apparent that progress *will* be made. Moreover, many of the advances that the motorcycle robot team perfects will likely be incorporated into other robots. In fact, it could be that these advances will be even more important than some of the advances fashioned by the winning team. (This is because the ability to keep the balance of a two-wheeled robot is far more difficult than a four-wheeled one. To the extent that robots need to occupy less space to become household fixtures, it could very well be that they will need to be taller and thinner than they are today and will need better balance.) Therefore, those failures that I and the others were laughing at—well, the joke could be on us because it could be Cal-Berkeley's technology that allows robotic technology to take off.

This would not be dissimilar to the many advances that some early aviation pioneers contributed to the progress of human flight. It is not now generally appreciated, but just a few short years after the Wright Brothers had achieved their historic flight, few of their breakthrough technologies were used in next-generation aircraft. Instead the technological advances of some of those who had failed earlier had progressed to the point where they were more valuable.

Exponential **INSIGHT**

From 1830 to 1840 the amount of railroad track laid in America increased tenfold to 2,808 miles and yet most Americans had still never seen a train. Between the Wright Brothers' historic flight on December 17, 1903, and 1905, the distance airplanes flew jumped from 120 feet to twenty-four miles— or more than the combined total of all the flights of 1904. Still, most Americans were not even aware that man had achieved human flight.

Extraordinary advances are being made in fields that you might not even be aware of. Before laughing at future predictions, one needs to understand what is going on in these areas first or the joke could be on you.

JUMP THE CURVE STRATEGY #38:
Mine History for Pearls of Wisdom

It is hard to fathom now, but once upon a time pearls were among the most valued of commodities. They were known as the "queen of gems" and even played a starring role in the most expensive banquet in human history.

According to some historical reports, in 41 B.C. Mark Antony, then one of the rulers of Rome, summoned Cleopatra to Tarsus (in present-day Turkey) to question her about her possible involvement in the assassination of Julius Caesar three years before. (Other historians suggest he merely wanted her support for an upcoming military campaign.)

As was Cleopatra's way, she arrived in a lavish ship and proceeded to wine and dine Mark Antony for a few days. At one point she wagered Antony that she could throw the most expensive dinner in history.

After the meal in question was nearing it end, Antony remarked that while it was good, it wasn't noticeably more lavish than any of the previous banquets she had staged. Thereupon, Cleopatra removed one of the large pearl earrings she was wearing, dissolved it into a goblet of wine vinegar, and proceeded to drink it.

The pearl was so rare and large that Cleopatra said it was worth "10,000,000 sesterces"—or the value of fifteen countries. Whether this was the exact value or a bit of diplomatic hyperbole is unknown, but it is fair to say that the pearl was worth a lot because Antony conceded defeat.

Today, of course, pearls—even pearls the size of Cleopatra's earrings—have nowhere near their former value. The reason? At the beginning of the twentieth century, a couple of gentlemen in Japan discovered that oysters could be made to produce pearls of higher quality and perfect shape by seeding a core—or a nuclei—into the oyster and letting the oyster take care of the rest. These pearls became known as "cultured" pearls, and today they are the foundation of an industry that is, pardon the pun, a shell of its former self.

And what has replaced pearls as the queen of gems? While they don't bear the same title, the new kid on the block is a girl's best friend—the diamond. The largest one in the world, with an estimated value of $130 million, is the famed Millennium Star.

Is it possible that a girl's best friend could go the way of the queen of gems? The answer is an unqualified yes, and the technology that could prove to be the diamond's undoing is suspiciously similar to that which produced the cultured pearl. At the present time, one company—Apollo Diamond—is seeding a small diamond core and growing two-carat diamonds synthetically through a process known as chemical vapor deposition. With no sense of historical irony, the existing diamond industry, in an attempt to thwart Apollo's progress, has requested that federal regulators mandate that the company refer to its product as "cultured" diamonds.

From the perspective of the diamond industry, here is what is so troubling about these diamonds. Not only are they molecularly identical to the diamonds that DeBeers and other diamond companies harvest from the earth, they are actually better in the sense that they don't have *any* molecular imperfections. In fact, the surest way for jewelry experts to discern a synthetic diamond from one harvested from the earth is that the former are better than natural diamonds.

Equally impressive, these manmade diamonds have the advantage of being produced over the course of a couple of days—unlike DeBeers and others who can only take from the earth what Mother Nature has produced over the course of the past 4 billion years. Furthermore, Apollo's technology will get better, faster, larger, and, ultimately, less expensive. As it does, diamonds—like natural pearls of the past—could become so inexpensive as to become almost an afterthought.

Unlikely you say? I don't think so. Simply consider the environmental degradation that diamond mining causes. According to the industry's own spokespeople, more than 250,000 tons of earth must be mined to produce a single one-carat diamond. Moreover, the exploitation of human labor—which continues to this day in many parts of Africa—remains a very real and disturbing issue. As consumers become more sensitive to the human and environmental costs of natural diamonds, it is easy to envision a future where people are willing to pay more for "cultured" diamonds not only on the basis of price and quality, but for ethical and environmental reasons as well.

The point of this story is to show how technology has a way of making once-expensive items affordable. Consider data storage. Fifty years ago it would have cost a person $3,200 a month to rent a device capable of storing five megabytes of information. Today a memory stick with 1,000 times that capacity can be purchased for $29.

Another example is the personal computer. Just sixty years ago researchers at the University of Pennsylvania constructed the world's first computer. It occupied 1,800 square feet, weighed three tons, consisted of 19,000 vacuum tubes, and cost half a million dollars. Today your laptop computer is thousands of times more powerful, can be purchased for less than a $1,000, and is about the size of a book.

Change, they say, is inevitable. In the exponential economy large-scale change is inevitable. But this does not imply a shortage of business opportunities. If anything it implies just the opposite.

Let's review the two previous examples. If someone had told IBM officials in 1956, when 5 MB of storage cost $3,200 a month, that someday a company (such as Google) would give away 2.8 gigabytes of storage for free, they likely would have wondered how any company could survive in such a cutthroat environment. Of course, the industry is a tough one in which to survive, but Seagate, SanDisk and others are doing just fine because new uses and applications requiring vast amounts of data storage became feasible, commonplace, and widely desired.

The same is true with computing. The personal computer, software, the Internet, iPods, cell phones, and search engines were all enabled by the changing economics of the semiconductor industry.

Exponential **INSIGHT**

The most immediate worry of those jewelers envisioning a world of manmade diamonds is the effect they will have on the value of existing diamonds. It is a natural concern, and people should plan accordingly. The exponential executive, however, is encouraged to think differently about how to jump the curve. Often the real opportunity lies not in knowing what the new technology will destroy but rather in what it will create. In the case of the manmade diamonds, some experts are already considering a new diamondoid age of biocompatible computer chips, superhard tools, and possibly even inexpensive building materials made out of diamonds. As the old saying goes, "when one door is closed, often another is opened."

JUMP THE CURVE STRATEGY #39:
Take Expert Advice with a Grain of Salt

Let us take one more trip back in time and explore the origins of the telephone. In 1876, on the same day that General George Custer was routed by Lakota and Northern Cheyenne warriors at the Battle of Little Bighorn, Alexander Graham Bell demonstrated the telephone in public for the first time. And while the event generated much excitement among the general public, it was met with a collective yawn from much of the establishment. President Rutherford B. Hayes commented at the time, "A wonderful invention but who would have ever want to use one?"

Not to be outdone by the president of the United States, the president of Western Union that same year dismissed the phone as an "electronic toy" and called Bell's proposal to put one in everyone's home "utterly out of the question."

For a considerable amount of time the Western Union official was correct. In 1900 a person had to physically travel to the phone company to make a long-distance call from New York to London, and it cost $100—then about half an average person's annual salary—to speak for ten minutes.

By 1980 phone technology had progressed to the point where nearly everyone had a phone in their home, and the cost of that same call to London was about ten bucks. Twenty years later many of us had cell phones, and that call only set us back $1. Today it is increasingly common to see people with voice-activated, Bluetooth cell phones that use Skype or other VoIP software to make calls for free.

Now let us return to the Western Union president's quote. The notion of a phone in every home was not utterly preposterous. What was utterly preposterous is that Western Union's telegraph business—which delivered as many as 200 million messages annually in 1929—survived as long as it did. In early 2006, unable to compete with text-messaging teenagers and other communication devices, the company posted a short sentence on its Web site. It read: "Effective January 27, 2006, Western Union will discontinue all Telegram and Commercial Messaging services."

Exponential INSIGHT

Today all sorts of dreamers suggest all sorts of wild-eyed ideas. For instance, some people predict that solar cells will soon cover the roof of every home and business in America. Others suggest that robots will be as common as computers, and still others estimate that in the near future nanoscale devices will soon be patrolling our bodies, searching out and destroying cancer and other deadly diseases at their earliest stages. If one follows how technology is making certain visions cheaper, it becomes easier to understand how such things might come to fruition. At a minimum, to jump the curve it is best to take with a healthy dose of salt the words of those who are the beneficiaries or guardians of the status quo.

Will the same thing happen to some of today's bigger industries? Yes. Let's just consider one: the medical diagnostic industry. Look at the trends. To diagnose disease today people often have to travel to a hospital and undergo a series of expensive procedures that use expensive equipment and rely on highly trained medical professionals to operate.

Advances are already on the way to produce low-cost devices that doctors can keep in their offices that will rapidly and accurately test for hundreds of diseases. Soon even cheaper devices—perhaps even small computer chips capable of being placed inside the human body—will alert people of the presence of some new disease—and do it all from the comfort of one's home.

Unlikely you say? Perhaps, but is the scenario any more unlikely than someone predicting 100 years ago that in the future people would make voice-activated telephone calls halfway around the world from the comfort of their automobile, for free?

JUMP THE CURVE STRATEGY #40:
Bet on the Machine

In December 2006, Vladimir Kramnik, the world's reigning chess champion, was defeated in a six-game match by Deep Fritz—a computer—by the score of four games to two. It was quite likely the last time that such a highly publicized chess match pitting man against machine will take place. This is because, as one leading computer scientist put it, "the science is done."

The science is done. Since Kramnik last played Deep Fritz in 2002, when he battled the computer to an honorable 4-4 draw, his Elo rating—which measures the relative strength of a chess player—dropped slightly. During the same period, Deep Fritz bolstered the number of positions it could calculate per second from 2.7 million to 8 million.

This, of course, is not the first time the science has been "done." In 1910 the American Automobile Association sponsored a match between a Maxwell Model Q touring car with a 22-horsepower engine and a horse and buggy. The event was billed at the time as the "first official cost test ever held between an automobile and a horse and a wagon," and it was designed to ease people's concerns over the cost-effectiveness and efficiency of the automobile.

It was no contest. The car covered 458 miles in six days and recorded thirteen miles to the gallon. The horse covered only 197 miles, and because a direct comparison in terms of fuel consumed was not feasible, it was noted that the horse required twelve quarts of oats and twenty pounds of hay for every thirty miles it covered. (No one considered it necessary at the time to conduct an environmental impact assessment regarding the amount of carbon dioxide released into the atmosphere by the automobile versus the amount of manure left on the roadside.)

The theme of man versus machine is not a new one. Many of us are familiar with the story of John Henry, the railroad worker who pitted himself against the steam powered drill in a race to determine who could clear away the most mountainside for the railroad track.

The legend is quite instructive. For thirty-five minutes John Henry drilled away with two twenty-pound hammers—one in each hand—while the railroad foreman operated the newfangled steam drill. At the end of the contest Henry had drilled two seven-foot holes (for a total of fourteen feet) compared to one nine-foot hole for the steam drill.

Sweet revenge, right? After all, the human won. Yes, but recall Henry collapsed a minute later—the victim of burst blood vessel in his brain.

Does this mean resistance is futile against all machines? Of course not. People and businesses simply need to adapt and adjust. Many jobs of yesterday have been relegated to the ash heap of history. Just a century ago, close to 50 percent of the American population lived and worked on farms. Today that figure is less than 2 percent.

Forty years ago, the number of telephone switchboard operators stood at 420,000. Now it is a dying job category. Today travel agents are being displaced by the Internet, optometrists by Lasik surgery, and in 2006 it was estimated that more than 35 percent of all prostatectomies were performed by robots. Does this mean doctors are next? To be sure, some will be replaced, but it is just as likely that robots will allow average surgeons to perform like great surgeons, and the great ones will become superstars. The exponential executive must focus on how some of these new emerging technologies can help them do their existing jobs better while at the same time open up new possibilities.

The pace of change is hastening. In January 2007 a story in the *London Times* reported that two companies were experimenting with robots to build homes. A couple of salient points from the article are worth considering. First, the article noted that robots could perform some tasks *200 times faster* than a person. Secondly, as one expert pointed out, "Years ago shoes, shirts, and automobiles were all made by hand." Today they are not. In his words, "it doesn't make sense" to build houses by hand.

He is right; it doesn't make sense. Just as it no longer makes sense to have half the population working on the farm or devote 400,000 people to switching telephone calls. In an interesting exercise in 1994, an official at the U.S. Census Bureau noted that if the number of telephone calls had increased to its present level (then

86 billion) but no corresponding advances had been made in technology during the same period, exactly 3,564,607 phone operators would be needed to handle that volume of phone traffic.

Exponential **INSIGHT**

In many ways, the history of warfare is the history of technology. The knife, the sword, the spear, the bow and arrow, the gun, the tank, the airplane, and the satellite all revolutionized warfare in one way or another. What's next? It's impossible, of course, to predict, but the advent of robotic technology bears close watching. As was mentioned earlier, the U.S. Department of Defense is dedicating a sizeable portion of its $132 billion Future Combat Systems budget to the development of robots in the expectation that these machines will comprise one-third of the United States' fighting force by 2015. To the extent that many past technologies invented by the military have gone on to shape the rest of society (the computer, satellites, the Internet, and so on), robotics are probably a prudent way to "bet on the machine" in the near future.

JUMP THE CURVE STRATEGY #41:
Develop a Future Bias

Among its many other implications, the accelerating rate change means that the amount of change society will experience within the next twenty years will be the equivalent of the amount of change we have experienced in the past 100 years. A quick walk back in time will reveal that the amount of progress in the past century has been nothing short of extraordinary.

In 1907, 50 percent of people lived and worked on farms, there were only a few thousands automobiles on the road, and life expectancy was a mere forty-seven years. Today we are living, on average, to eighty years, over 1 billion cars populate the planet, and less than 2 percent of the population works in agriculture.

As Steve Jurvetson, a leading venture capitalist in Silicon Valley, has said, the change that is coming our way will require people to be accepting of the "embarrassing and futuristic." What Jurvetson is really saying is that people need to keep a very open mind with regard to the future, and they need to have the courage to confront conventional wisdom and to stand up to peer pressure when others laugh or dismiss futuristic ideas as fundamentally preposterous.

One way to do this is to formulate what I call a *future bias*. A future bias is the opposite of a *hindsight bias*, which is defined as the notion that once an event happens people tend to give themselves far more credit for having thought the event would happen than they actually did.

For instance, by 1915 most people gave themselves credit for thinking that human flight would occur within their lifetime. A poll of 1900, however, would likely have revealed that few people actually believed such an event would occur. The *New York Times*, only days before the Wright Brothers' historic achievement, dismissed human flight in an editorial saying, "A man-carrying airplane will eventually be built but only if mathematicians and engineers work steadily for the next one to ten million years."

A future bias means being open to the idea that exponential changes in computers, bandwidth, biotechnology, nanotechnology, and the cognitive sciences are converging in such a manner that the world of 2028 will be as different from 2008 as today is from 1908.

Exponential INSIGHT

New technologies are often seen as the purview of the rich. For instance, the earliest automobiles were often little more than toys for the wealthy. Over time, new technological advances, new manufacturing methods, and economies of scale converged to bring cars to the masses. One way to develop a future bias is to consider what is expensive today but might someday be within the reach of the common person. One example that comes to mind is space flight. In 2007 Charles Simonyi, a multibillionaire, and Anousheh Ansari forked over between $20 and $25 million each to visit the International Space Station for a period of ten to thirteen days. If you think you'll never fly in space, consider this: Do you think your ancestors at the turn of the twentieth century ever thought they would own two or maybe even three cars—not just in their lifetime but at the same time? Things become more plausible if one maintains a future bias.

CONCLUSION

Like a modern-day John Henry, there are many things humans are still better at than computers, but if you place a long bet on machines you can jump the curve by considering which industries and jobs will be on the losing end of those bets. If it's the case that the next twenty years will see the equivalent of a hundred years of progress, then we will need to go back to school because we have a lot to learn. And we might have even more to unlearn, which is the subject of our next chapter.

The illiterate of the twenty-first century will not be those who cannot read and write, but those who cannot learn, unlearn, and relearn.

—Alvin Toffler

In a time of drastic change, it is the learners who inherit the future. The learned find themselves equipped to live in a world that no longer exists.

—Eric Hoffer

In some sense our ability to open the future will depend not on how well we learn anymore but on how well we are able to unlearn.

—Alan Kay

CHAPTER 10

Learning to Unlearn

The three quotes listed on the facing page are all really variations on the same theme. And, to be honest, the idea is an old one and is perhaps best captured by Mark Twain, who said more than a century and a half ago while he was toiling away on the Mississippi River as a boat pilot:

> Two things seemed pretty apparent to me. One was that in order to be a pilot a man had to learn more than any one man ought to learn; and the other was that he must learn it all over again in a different way every 24 hours.

What Twain recognized is that the fundamental condition in his environment was *change*, and he understood that if he wanted to first survive and prosper it was imperative that he master this context. To do so, he instinctively grasped that it wasn't simply enough to know a lot, he also had to *unlearn* some things and relearn them in the context of his changing environment.

That is precisely the predicament that today's leaders and exponential executives find themselves in. But the challenge is much harder than is generally recognized. Why is this? In part it is because humans are conditioned to optimize what we know and add to it. It is not in our nature to discard old knowledge or throw it away.

Thomas Kuhn, in his book *The Structure of Scientific Revolutions*, which was deemed one of the most influential books of the twentieth century, discussed how it is that paradigms—defined as conventional ways of viewing the world and trying to solve problems—can and do change over time. One of the keys to managing this change, Kuhn wrote, was that "at times of revolution, when normal scientific tradition changes, the scientist's perception of his environment must be reeducated—in some familiar situations he must learn to see a new gestalt."

One of the tricky things about exponential growth, as been mentioned before but bears repeating, is that in the beginning it is almost indistinguishable from linear growth. Recall the example of the lily pad.

Think of day one, with the development of the printing press, as being the beginning. Day ten marked the creation of the steam engine. Day twenty saw the invention of the telephone and day twenty-three the advent of the integrated circuit. Recall that day twenty-six is when the growth curve finally begins to slope noticeably upward. Since 1947 we have experienced the personal computer, the cell phone, and the Internet. Yet we are still only at day twenty-five. To be sure, society has experienced an extraordinary amount of change in the past few "days," and to a number of people and businesses—many of whom who been widely successful—they might be forgiven for thinking that this growth has been nothing more than fast linear growth. But that just isn't true.

The amount of change that society will experience in the near future is nothing short of revolutionary. As Thomas Kuhn reminds us, during times of revolution we "must learn to see a new gestalt." That new gestalt is exponential growth.

JUMP THE CURVE STRATEGY #42:
Take a Class in Unlearning 101

How does one learn a new gestalt? To begin, one must start by unlearning some things. But what things do we unlearn? For our purposes, a good place to start would be to imagine what a course on unlearning what might look like.

One place to start is to imagine where the course would take place. Initially it will be—and already is—online. In January 2007 the Massachusetts Institute of Technology announced that it was putting all of its courses online for free—for anyone in the world to access.

And let's remember, the online classroom is only going to get better. The Internet of the future will be streaming incredible amounts of data-rich information anywhere in the world, students will be capable of wirelessly downloading the latest information from flexible electronic books that display both the written word and video files, and new software programs will be capable of translating text from Mandarin Chinese, French, or Farsi into English—and vice versa.

Another place a course on unlearning might gravitate toward is 3-D virtual-reality environments such as Linden Labs' Second Life—a site where anyone can create a personal avatar of himself, meet other virtual avatars, and engage in online training sessions. As of this writing IBM, Dell, Intel, Circuit City, and Sears have all created a virtual presence in Second Life.

Interestingly one of the initial motives of this move was not to create a stronger presence on the Internet (although that is certainly a factor), it was to achieve cost savings on employee education, as was explained in the Chapter 4: Walk the Escalator.

What is more interesting from the perspective of unlearning is how Second Life and other virtual-reality sites can be exploited to provide people with different perspectives. In a virtual environment, people can take on any appearance they want. While some people will undoubtedly use it for escapist fantasies, it could also be a powerful tool to help people unlearn certain habits. Imagine, for example, customer service representatives or managers being required to act as customers in one of their own online stores. The experience could provide a unique and refreshing perspective.

Longer term, the classroom of unlearning will likely become even more immersive. Perhaps Second Life will morph into Third Life. Among the technologies this environment are likely to incorporate will be enhanced visual, auditory, voice and speech recognition, and haptic technologies. Doctors and service technicians could use these tools to practice operations and repairs *in silico* before being allowed to ply their trade in the real world.

These tools will also be a boon for learning, unlearning, and relearning. People are often classified into one of three broad categories of learning: visual, auditory, or kinesthetic. Visual people learn by seeing or reading something, auditory learners by hearing it, and kinesthetic learners learn by doing it with their hands and muscles. (It is not quite this simple. Many people use a combination of different techniques for different things, but in general, most people tend to favor one of the three methods over the other two.)

A course on unlearning could exploit these natural tendencies and help people absorb new ways of doing things. For instance, instead of just reading about how a new drug works on a cancer patient, doctors could watch how it interacts with and disables a cancer cell. Other businesses could use such immersive technology to gain a deeper appreciation of what an elderly person experiences and create products that better address their needs.

Many courses on unlearning won't have a teacher. They will rather be open source in nature, and the content will not be provided by a single "expert" but instead it will be continually added to and improved upon by a vast collection of people. To this end, a new wiki called Curriki has recently been created. Its goal is to support the development and free distribution of world-class educational material to anyone who needs it—anywhere in the world.

But far from being a shoddy collection of disjointed or inferior ideas, the result of these wikis will be vastly superior to anything a single expert could pull together. In the case of business wikis, they will contain advice and insights from employees, suppliers, and customers.

Among the adjustments this will require is that managers will need to unlearn their own reliance on experts. People will need to unlearn the idea that money and quality are synonymous. In the future, many of the best products will be the creation of open-source methods and wikis.

Another thing people will have to unlearn is that there isn't always an answer. This is because so many fields are constantly evolving. An admission of one's own ignorance may well be the first step most people will need to take upon entering the unlearning classroom of the future. Exponential executives may even have to go a step farther and accept that ignorance will be the largest element in their future educational needs.

THE HISTORY OF THE WORLD IN FIFTY YEARS

In his famous speech at Rice University where he declared that it was America's intention to put a man on the moon by the end of the decade, President Kennedy said "[t]he greater our knowledge increases, the greater our ignorance unfolds," adding that "the vast stretches of the unknown and the unanswered and the unfinished still far outstrip our collective comprehension."

Kennedy went on to offer a historical perspective for the magnitude of change society had experienced over the short course of human history. He asked his audience to condense the 50,000 years of man's recorded history into the span of fifty years. Under this scenario, Kennedy noted that not much happened for the first forty years. Ten years ago, man emerged from his cave, and only five years ago did he learned to write. Christianity appeared two years ago, the printing press this year, and just two months ago the steam engine appeared. Last month electric lights, telephones, automobiles, and airplanes became available, and only last week did we develop penicillin, television, and nuclear weapons. To reach "the stars before midnight tonight," Kennedy then poignantly added that Americans would have to "dispel old [and] new ignorance."

Since achieving Kennedy's goal in 1969, progress has continued exponentially. Taking his historical analogy a little further, in the last proverbial day computers, biotechnology, the Internet, and the sequencing of the human genome have all appeared on the scene. What this model implies is that the exponential executive will need to continue to "dispel old ignorance," only do it on a faster scale.

JUMP THE CURVE STRATEGY #43:
Put on a Different Hat

Earlier in the book I recounted how knowledge was doubling every seven years and pointed out that if this trend continues everything known today will represent just 1 percent of the sum total of world knowledge in 2050. Consider then how a significantly better understanding of the human brain might influence not just science but economics. For instance, we know that, contrary to most economic theory, many people do not always act rationally when it comes to making spending and investing decisions. What will a better understanding of the brain portend for decision-making in this regard?

The answer is likely to be quite a lot. Take the following example. If given a choice between winning $150 or losing $100 on a coin flip (that is, where the odds of heads or tails are equal), many people refuse the deal because they *fear* the prospect of losing $100 more than they appreciate the benefit of gaining $150. This is the case even though the game is strongly tilted in their favor. The chances are that you will win $75 ($150×.5) versus losing $50 ($100×.5)—and this means that if you played the game ten times on average you would win $250. Still, most people are reluctant to even accept the bet over ten attempts. What is at work here is something called *loss aversion*, and it demonstrates that, contrary to rational economic theory, people can and still do make bad decisions—frequently.

A second example involves gift receipts. When people are asked if they would prefer to be given a $15 gift receipt to Amazon. com today or receive a $20 gift receipt in two weeks, a surprising number select the first choice in spite of the long-term economic advantages of the second option. What scientists have discovered is that in both this instance and the coin-flipping example there is a disproportionate amount of activity in the limbic area of the brain. Neuroeconomics suggests that such information might be useful in determining how to help people make better long-term decisions such as preparing for retirement.

What else might change as a result of an enhanced understanding of the human brain? For one thing, marketing will. After the 2007 Super Bowl, in which advertisers plunked down a healthy $2.6 million for a thirty-second spot, researchers at UCLA showed that Coca-Cola's commercials scored the best at connecting with peoples' emotions and leaving them with a positive feeling. It obtained this information by using functional magnetic resonance imaging (fMRI) to watch how people's brains responded to ads.

If neuromarketing is the next wave, it might, among other things, require marketing executives for beer companies to unlearn the notion that scantily clad women, talking frogs, or funny shots of a young man getting hit in the groin are neither the best nor the only way to sell their product.

Medicine is another field ripe for an information explosion. In many instances doctors are today treating some diseases on the basis of limited information. As the connections between the brain and other parts of the body, including the human heart, become better understood, new methods of treatment are sure to arise. Similarly the relationship of whether a disease is the result of genetic or environmental factors, at present, is also only vaguely appreciated. As new findings come to light, many of these relationships will be better understood. This will require medical professionals to unlearn old ways of practicing their profession and relearn new ones.

A perfect example is the case of Barry Marshall. In the early 1980s he was a practicing physician in Australia with virtually no research experience. Still, he became convinced that ulcers were caused not by stress and spicy food but by bacteria called *Helicobacter pylori*. When he presented his theory before a conference of experts in Brussels in 1983 he was practically laughed off the podium. To make a long story short, in 1994 the National Institute of Health concluded that most ulcers were caused by the bacteria, and in 2005 Marshall and his colleague Robin Warren were awarded the Nobel Prize in Medicine. (A staggering number of ulcer sufferers are still unaware that antibiotics can cure them, but that's another problem.)

To bring it back to a slightly more practical level, we know some lessons on unlearning are already out there. Anyone who has read Michael Lewis's superb book *Money Ball* knows that Billy Beane, the general manager of the Oakland Athletics, has been able to keep his team consistently competitive by unlearning the baseball business.

Instead of relying on the subjective opinions of crusty old baseball scouts who have spent their lives around the game and claim they can spot the next "phenom" from a mile away, Beane replaced many of them with Ivy League graduates who can crunch players' statistics on their laptop computers using sophisticated statistical models and complex algorithms. In so doing he has been able to make George Steinbrenner, who thinks nothing of spending $160 million annually in an attempt to get back to the World Series, look foolish for the past six years.

Exponential INSIGHT

Lest one thinks that there aren't many opportunities to unlearn things, let us quickly look at a second example. In *The Wisdom of Crowds*, James Surowiecki points out that David Romer, an economist at Berkeley, used statistical probabilities to determine whether NFL coaches would have been better off going for a touchdown on fourth and goal or kicking a field goal. What he discovered is nothing short of startling. In 1,100 different situations where he determined the coach would have been better off going for it, the coaches opted to kick it 992 times. Eighty-eight percent of the time they made the wrong choice!

Why would NFL coaches make the wrong decision almost nine out of ten times? A big part of the answer is loss aversion. They are afraid of losing three points. The purpose of the game, however, is to win, and by unlearning some old things and relearning new things NFL coaches can jump the curve. Exponential executives can do the same thing by adopting different ways of thinking about old problems.

It is with some irony then that another good quote on unlearning comes from Satchel Paige, who once said, "It's not what you don't know that hurts you. It's what you know that just ain't so."

A lot of baseball minds *think* they know what makes a great hitter or a great pitcher. Unfortunately the continued failure of certain managers and teams strongly suggests that Mr. Paige was right. A lot of what they think they know "just ain't so."

JUMP THE CURVE STRATEGY #44:
Ask New Questions

Albert Einstein once said that "sometimes the first step to solving an old problem is to ask a new question." Yet learning to ask new questions can be surprisingly difficult. Anyone who has ever grown up skiing and then tried to learn how to snowboard has probably experienced this and spent the better part of a day (or in my case two days) on his rear end. The two skills look basically the same—just as gliding looks similar to flying and kayaking to canoeing—yet switching from one activity to the other requires that old techniques be abandoned and new ones learned in order to achieve the same outcome. To be successful at a new skill—be it moving down a mountain, guiding a plane through the air, or propelling a vessel across open water—one often needs to ask and answer a new set of questions in order to reach the same outcome. For instance, for the snowboard to go downhill the skier needs to ask herself not "where do I point my board" but "where do I shift my weight."

The exponential economy will require many such new questions. For example, our increasingly mobile lifestyle caused one architect to ask an unusual question: Why have our buildings remained so steadfastly anchored to the ground when we ourselves are so mobile? Jennifer Siegal's question caused her to create prefabricated structures that can more easily react and respond to people's changing conditions. Advances in biotechnology will likely make people and industries ask and answer new questions about aging, and progress in rapid prototype manufacturing and nanotechnology will require manufacturers to ask whether the old methods of building things are still the most appropriate.

One company that has asked a new set of questions is Nintendo. For years the video-game manufacturer had been losing market share to Sony's PlayStation and Microsoft's Xbox. But rather than attempt to compete with those companies by bringing better and more powerful graphics to video gaming, Nintendo executives began asking a new set of questions, starting with: What does the nongamer want?

By asking this question the company found that many people who didn't play video games simply wanted games that were easier to use, didn't require hours to play, and weren't based in the fantasy scenarios so common to other video games. The result was Wii—a hand-held video game that is easy to use and appeals to gamers and nongamers alike. If the 2007 sales are any indication, it will be a huge hit.

Thomas Kuhn once wrote, "What a man sees depends both upon what he looks at and also upon what his previous visual-conceptional experience has taught him to see." He described how for more than ninety years a number of astronomers had spotted Uranus and noted that it had many planetary-like qualities, but they all refused to identify it as a planet because they were looking for stars. In fact, the first person to not identify it as a star still misidentified Uranus as a comet.

However, once astronomers began asking a different set of questions they soon identified Uranus for what it was—a planet. More interestingly, after this shift in questioning occurred astronomers began to ask if a number of other celestial orbs might not also be planets. Once they did, they identified some twenty additional planets over the course of the next fifty years. (These "planets" are not planets as most of us learned in grade school. They are large, nonround asteroids located in the Kuiper Belt.)

Exponential **INSIGHT**

This particular jump-the-curve tactic brings to mind that old adage, "If all you have is a hammer, everything looks like a nail." It just so happens that even the humble nail recently received a substantial makeover after 200 years because an engineer named Ed Sutt began asking new questions about why some houses were collapsing in the face of hurricane winds. What Sutt learned is that in many instances the nail—not the construction of the home or the material—was to blame for a house collapsing.

By asking a series of new questions about every aspect of the nail, he then devised a new nail that has a bigger head, barbed rings, and is made out of a new alloy. Most importantly, the new nail can withstand hurricane winds of up to 170 miles per hour. To jump the curve, sometimes the exponential executive can hit the nail on the head by simply asking a series of smaller questions.

JUMP THE CURVE STRATEGY #45:
Fail Faster and Dare to Succeed Unconventionally

In today's accelerating environment, so many new technologies are advancing and converging with one another that it is not practical to expect every new initiative to work. It is not possible to stand still, however. Therefore, as Sir Francis Bacon once said, "If we are to achieve results never before accomplished, we must employ methods never before attempted."

One such method is to fail faster. Hector Ruiz, CEO of Advanced Micro Devices—a leading computer chip maker— expressed this philosophy well when he said that he doesn't mind if his people get ticketed for speeding; he just doesn't want them getting parking tickets.

Another community that has the right mentality in this regard is the venture capital industry. In general, nine out of every ten investments a venture capital firm makes will result in failure. The key to success is to make the few victories that are achieved asymmetrical. That is, if you only have a 10 percent chance at success, you'd better make sure the payouts of those few victories are extraordinarily high.

An important side benefit of this approach is that misplaced bets and losses aren't just losses, they are also learning opportunities. Josh Wolfe, the editor of *The Forbes/Wolfe Nanotech Newsletter*, writes a splendid weekly column entitled "The Nanotech Insider," and a few years ago he recounted a good story about an art teacher that aptly captured this idea.

The teacher asked two groups to construct some pottery pieces. The instructor told one group to focus on just quality and the other to focus on quantity. At the end of the exercise he assessed both groups on quality and found that the one focused on quantity actually created the higher-quality pieces of art.

The reason? With each new piece—however imperfect—the group was learning something new. Or as Henry Ford once said, "Failure is only the opportunity to begin again more intelligently."

It is also true that some things will have to be taken on faith in the exponential economy. Thomas Kuhn wrote, "The man who embraces a new paradigm at an early stage must often do so in defiance of the evidence provided by problem-solving. He must, that is, have faith that the new paradigm will succeed with the many large problems that confront it, knowing only that the older paradigm has failed. A decision of that kind can only be made on faith."

Brian Walker, the CEO of Herman Miller, the furniture manufacturer, expressed this sentiment when asked of his decision to take his company in a new direction. He said, "I don't know if I can explain this economically and in detail right now, but I believe that long term, if we are going to re-create ourselves again, we have to place some bets that are out of the ordinary."

Another example of unlearning can be found in the example of Larry Burns, vice president for research and development at General Motors, when he said, "I know fuel cells are a disruptive technology, but we have to attack ourselves." It was his way of acknowledging that the era of the internal combustion engine—a technology that has dominated the automotive industry for the past hundred years—is nearing its end, and in order for General Motors to survive it needs to "attack" itself.

Now, normally, attacking oneself might be viewed, at best, as counterintuitive and, at worst, self destructive. But this is precisely the type of thinking that executives and corporations need to employ if they are to survive in today's exponential economy.

Consider one last example from the world of sport. In April 1997 Tiger Woods won golf's most prestigious tournament, The Masters, by a record eleven strokes. It was his fourth victory in his past fifteen tournaments, and although he was only twenty-one years old, he was already being widely hailed as the best golfer ever.

Woods, however, was not content to rest on his laurels. He studied videotapes of his amazing Masters victory and came to a surprising conclusion: "My swing really sucks." He then proceeded to do something even more surprising. He reinvented his entire golf swing. Woods improved his strength and flexibility and completely changed his grip. He intuitively understood that although he was already an excellent golfer, he could be even better. In order to achieve that higher level, he needed to first risk getting worse in the short term.

Over the course of the next two years Woods won only one tournament. He was confident, though, that he was improving as a golfer. Time eventually proved him right. By early 1999 Woods was back on top of his game, and over the course of the next two years he rewrote the record books. He won ten of the next fourteen tournaments he entered, and at one time he simultaneously held the title to all four major golf tournaments.

Another strategy to enhance an organization's willingness to fail faster is to outsource projects. By outsourcing the riskiest jobs, managers can insulate employees from the consequences that often accompany projects when they fail. Such a step is often necessary, because few executives are willing to embrace Hector Ruiz's philosophy of encouraging speeding tickets (and then not penalizing people when they do get a ticket). Therefore, managers interested in generating new ideas and pushing the envelope should consider outsourcing many of their riskier projects.

Related to this idea of being more receptive to new ideas is the notion that you should accord people's positive responses to new projects and ideas the same weight given to negative comments. You might think that you already do this, but this is rarely the case. According to a landmark study conducted more than two decades ago by Professor Teresa Amabile, people who made negative or critical comments on new ideas and projects were judged by their peers to be smarter than those who offered praise. Amabile theorized people are hardwired to take no more seriously than yes. She believed this trait existed for evolutionary reasons because often negative stimulus—such as someone telling our ancestors not to go in that cave because there was a sabertooth tiger in it—could prevent death. But in this new environment of exponential change, the tables have flipped, and it is now the status quo that is the dangerous condition.

JUMP THE CURVE STRATEGY #46:
Change Your World View

Unlike most psychologists, Abraham Maslow studied healthy people, not sick ones. Maslow's hierarchy of needs, his seminal theory on human motivation, outlined a great many of the characteristics of a "self-actualized" person. Among the more notable characteristics were "a willingness to change one's view of the world" and "an ability to learn from anyone." He never identified either as unlearning, but a "willingness to change's one world view" comes pretty close to capturing that sentiment.

Maslow further noted that self-actualized individuals are unhampered by conventional wisdom and are prepared to be unpopular. He also said that they are willing to embrace a fresh rather than a stereotyped perspective of the world, were unfrightened of the unknown, and had a tendency to self explore. Again, all are suggestive of people who are willing to unlearn.

Exponential **INSIGHT**

Nobel Laureate Andre Gide once said, "Man cannot discover new oceans unless he has the courage to lose sight of the shore." It is also true, however, that when people lose their compass their natural reaction is to hug the shore. The problem becomes even more acute when a period such as the exponential economy is approaching. In this environment, what might seem like the riskiest strategy—pulling up the anchor and setting sail—is actually the safest. The moral: To survive in the exponential economy you might have to physically force yourself to take a position that requires you to change your view of the world.

CONCLUSION

Interestingly, the characteristic Maslow identified as being most central to self-actualized individuals is "a feeling of limitless horizons." This is a good thing too, because the implications of the exponential economy should give a person a "feeling of limitless horizons." In fact, many of the implications will sound downright impossible, but then that leads us to our final chapter: Doing the Impossible.

Alice laughed. "There's no use trying," she said; "one can't believe impossible things." "I daresay you haven't had much practice," said the Queen. "When I was younger, I always did it for half an hour a day. Why, sometimes I've believed as many as six impossible things before breakfast."

—Lewis Carroll, *Alice in Wonderland*

Research should be defined as something half the people think is impossible.

—Burt Rutan, winner of the $10 million X Prize and the first person to launch a privately owned airplane into space

CHAPTER 11

Doing the Impossible

As late as December 2001, a number of Web sites posted statements to the effect that it was impossible to fold a piece of paper more than seven times. The typical claim went something like this: No matter its size or thickness, no piece of paper can be folded in half more than seven times. If you try this experiment at home you would be inclined to believe this is true and might even be surprised that someone got that many. (In my own case I could only feebly fold the paper six times.)

Nevertheless, the links to these sites are now all expired. That is because in January 2002 Britney Gallivan, then a high-school junior, while in the process of solving an extra credit problem for a math class became the first person in the world to fold a piece of paper nine times. For good measure she then went on to do it a tenth, eleventh, and twelfth time. (Should you wish to read about this accomplishment in greater detail I encourage you to read her forty-page pamphlet, *How to Fold Paper in Half Twelve*

Times: An "Impossible" Challenge Solved and Explained, which is available from the Historical Society of Pomona, California.)

I open with this story because Ms. Gallivan's example of doing the impossible with a piece of paper segues quite nicely into another story that involves folding paper and includes some impossible-sounding numbers.

At a dinner party, I once posed the following question to my guests: "If it was theoretically possible to fold a piece of paper fifty times, how thick do you imagine the piece of paper would be after the fiftieth fold?" The responses from this unscientific sample ranged from a low of eight feet (the size of a bookshelf) to a height of two miles.

The latter response drew a few laughs and guffaws from the others around the table, but had this been *The Price is Right* that guest would have won the contest because her answer was the closest without going over. Alas, she would not have been accorded any bonus points for coming within a hair's breath of the correct answer. In fact, it might shock you to know that she was off by a nontrivial 61,999,998 miles. That is because the correct answer is approximately 100 million kilometers—or 62 million miles.

To most people this figure sounds absolutely impossible, but it isn't. If one starts with the assumption that the width of an average piece of paper is 0.01 millimeters thick, after the fiftieth doubling it would reach a full two-thirds of the way to sun.

Now, paper itself *can't* be folded fifty times, but that isn't the point. The point is that the doubling of anything—be it transistors, protein-folding simulations, or gene sequences—even if it can't double fifty times, can still lead to some outcomes that sound almost impossible. For instance, returning to the paper-folding example, how many would believe that after just thirty folds the height would already reach the outer limits of the earth's atmosphere?

Returning to earth, let's again consider the case of the transistor. In 2008 the number of transistors placed on a computer will have doubled thirty times. Will it reach fifty? Who knows. Most experts agree that it could fizzle out after the thirty-fifth iteration, but they also expect that something else, such as molecular electronics or even quantum computers, could take over after that. But even if it just doubles five more times from today's level of 500 million transistors that will take us to 32 billion transistors—which is sixty-four times more powerful than the computers society possesses today.

How is one to think of all the impossible things that might some day be possible as a result of such exponential advances? To begin, it helps by trying to think in a different dimension. If you are like me, you probably have a hard enough time grasping the notion of the time-space continuum as a fourth dimension, let alone imagining a fifth dimension. (Harder still is the idea that there might be up to ten, eleven, or even twenty-six different dimensions, as string theory posits.)

I had never been able to wrap my mind around this idea of different dimensions until I heard Michio Kaku, a theoretical physicist and cofounder of the string field theory, speak on the topic. During a radio interview a few years back he said that he came to conceptualize the idea of a new dimension while watching a carp swim in the pond.

Kaku said that he knew that if the carp were an engineer all it would believe in was water, and as an engineer it would only concern itself with matters of water because that was all that was around it. A carp physicist, however, Kaku reckoned, would at some point cast its eyes upward and see ripples on the water. When it did, it would wonder what was above those ripples.

So it should be with the exponential executive. There are ripples bubbling on the edges of science and technology today, and it is imperative that leaders begin thinking about what might lie beyond those ripples.

JUMP THE CURVE STRATEGY #47:
Swim Toward the Ripple

Consider the following paragraph:

> Dave Striver loved the university—its ivy-covered clock towers, its ancient and sturdy brick, and its sun-splashed verdant greens and eager youth. The university, contrary to popular opinion, is far from free of the stark, unforgiving trials of the business world: academia has its own tests, and some are as merciless as any in the marketplace of ideas. A prime example is the dissertation defense: to earn the Ph.D., to become a doctor, one must pass an oral examination on one's dissertation. This was the test Professor Edward Hart enjoyed giving.

As a writer, I think it is a fine piece of work and, like most good fiction, seems to possess an aura of real-world experience. Here's the problem—the paragraph was written by a computer program, dubbed StoryBook.

The program is designed to be, and I quote, "an end-to-end narrative prose generation system that uses narrative planning, sentence planning, a discourse history, lexical choice, revision, a full-scale lexicon and the well-known Fuf/Surge surface realizer."

If I engage in "lexical choice" as a writer I am not aware of it, and if the Fuf/Surge surface realizer is, indeed, well known, it has somehow escaped my attention. What has not failed to catch my attention is that this computer program is a ripple on the horizon of the world of writing.

I do not soon foresee a day when all writers will be replaced, but couple this with a recent advance made by software IBM engineers, who have created a program that can read two sentences and intelligently generate a third, and it is not difficult to imagine how computers could soon begin generating simple stories. It is possible to envision how some writers will be impacted. To this end, Thomson News is already using computers to generate news stories about companies' quarterly financial earnings a mere millisecond after a company posts its information to the Internet. Not surprisingly, this information is then being read and acted upon by computers at mutual funds and hedge funds, which are executing trades based on the information in these stories.

Similar scenarios are playing out in other professions. Many people are now able to draw up wills and other basic legal documents using low-cost software programs available over the Internet. What else does this particular ripple of computer-written prose suggest is on the horizon for the legal profession?

Let's consider for a moment a few of the other ripples glistening on the edges of tomorrow's economy. We will begin by taking a short walk back into history to January 25, 2005. On this day, a mere 106 years after Charles Duell was purported to have recommended closing the U.S. Patent Office because "everything that could be invented had been invented," the office issued patent number 7,117,186 for a specialized kind of circuitry. What made the patent so unique was that it was developed with the assistance of a genetic algorithm. This is slightly more surprising when you realize that to be awarded a patent an invention must demonstrate a nonobvious step—or a break from established practices. In essence, the patent proved that an artifical computer program had enough common sense to make a leap in logic.

The man behind the computer is John Koza, a professor at Stanford University, and what he has done is figure out how to marry genetic algorithms with artificial intelligence. The combination means, among other things, that he has automated the creative process.

In another case, Koza used his genetic program to "evolve" a better wide-field eyepiece for a telescope. Starting from scratch, in just 295 mutations his program constructed a telescope that possessed a view 10 degrees wider than a humanly patented telescope.

This idea of being able to see 10 degrees more is a good metaphor, because to see many of the other ripples that are shimmering on the surface of the exponential economy the exponential executive will best be served by seeing things from a slightly wider angle. And some of the things on the outer edges will surprise you.

For instance, Volkswagen has already created a car, the Golf GTI "53 Plus 1" that can drive itself at speeds up to 150 mph. I wouldn't yet recommend taking this "Herbie-on-steroids" for a spin quite yet, but the technology is only going to improve, and as it does it has the potential to revolutionize transportation.

So too does the SkyCar, a Jetson-like flying car that its inventor, Paul Moller, has been working on for almost four decades. His company now has a crude working prototype, and it expects the initial cost of its SkyCars to be in the neighborhood of $800,000 to $1 million. That sounds expensive—and it is—but we should consider that today many high-end consumers think nothing of plunking down a couple hundred thousand dollars for a Maybach or some other high-end luxury car. Further, economies of scale and other technological advances will likely lower the price over time. Once we take these things into consideration, flying cars become a ripple that could create some serious waves in the future—and not just in the field of transportation but for the travel industry and the real-estate industry.

On the energy front, equally startling ripples are emerging. Advances in clean coal, cellulosic ethanol, wind, geothermal energy, wave power, fuel cells, and even nuclear fusion technology are all very exciting and have great potential. But the fact remains that a giant fusion machine already exists, and it is sitting 93 million miles from earth. Moreover, every day it strikes the planet with 10,000 times the amount of energy that it needs. The device I refer to, of course, is the sun, and a variety of emerging technologies are being developed to harvest solar power in vast, affordable quantities.

Some energy experts point out that to meet the world's energy needs with existing solar technology would require solar cells totaling the size of the state of Oklahoma. Such a possibility sounds absurd. That is until one considers that a number of nanotechnology companies are on the verge of printing out solar cells that are thin as wallpaper and can be wrapped over the roofs of millions of homes, businesses, and other structures all around the world. If one totaled up the amount of space such flexible solar cells could cover, one might find that it still won't exceed an area the size of Oklahoma but it will be getting closer.

Today the world receives less than one-tenth of 1 percent of its energy from solar power. If that number were to increase 40 percent annually for the next decade, it would suggest through the power of zenzizenzizenzic that in ten years the world could meet almost 20 percent of its energy needs through solar power.

Is this likely to happen? I don't know. But it is certainly possible, and it is a ripple worth considering. Even if solar power doesn't grow as fast as I have suggested, such advances still have the power to shift the existing paradigms in transportation and energy.

There's an opportunity here for the exponential executive to jump the curve but it will require them to imagine the world of possibilities that will exist when energy is taken off the grid and people can begin producing much of their own energy from virtually anywhere on the planet.

If you can stretch your imagination and look 10 degrees in another direction, the view becomes even more amazing. Were you aware, for instance, that the seventy-seventh richest country in terms of gross national product—larger than the island nation of St. Vincent—is EverQuest.

Never heard of EverQuest? Perhaps that is because it can't be reached by car, boat, airplane, or even a SkyCar. In fact, it isn't even a real destination and can only be reached via your computer. It is a massively multiplayer online role-playing game (MMORPG) in which people can acquire skills and possessions that can then be bartered or sold on online auction sites like eBay for real money.

The rise of games such as EverQuest and the growing popularity of virtual-reality venues such as Second Life will only grow larger in the near future. As more people, products, and businesses move into these environments, real-world business opportunities are going to emerge as well. Today only a handful of people have figured out how to make their livelihood in Ever-Quest by designing digital castles and other highly coveted items and selling them on eBay for real money, but as next-generation developments enhance the Web and increase the amount, type, and format of information that can be sent over the Internet, this could change dramatically. Moreover, as haptic technology becomes more proficient and less expensive and more types of information become digitized, the possibilities will continue to increase, as will the opportunities for people and businesses to do things in this new, immersive milieu.

The famous economist John Maynard Keynes once quipped that "it is better to ship around recipes than it is to ship cake and biscuits"—meaning that the most efficient method of commerce is to trade information rather than physical objects. He was right, of course, but what happens when those recipes become molecular in nature? For instance, a pharmaceutical drug is nothing more than a specific set of molecules. In the future, rather than having drugs manufactured at a large facility it may be more practial for your local pharmacist to simply receive the molecular recipe from your doctor and manufacture the drug on the spot. This scenario becomes even more plausible when one considers how an enhanced understanding of the human genome portends an era of personalized medicine where drugs may be precisely tailored to your individual needs.

Let's explore briefly some of the ripples occurring in the fields of rapid prototype manufacturing, robotics, and nanotechnology. Dr. Adrian Bowyer, a senior lecturer in mechanical engineering at the University of Bath in the United Kingdom, has invented a device he calls the RepRap. It is a self-replicating rapid proto-typer, and it can print out copies of plates, dishes, combs, musical instruments, and, possibly, even copies of itself. It is intended to deliver a low-cost manufacturing method to many parts of the developing world that lack the infrastructure to produce and transport such items.

At the present time, the device is estimated to cost $45,000 and has a limited repertoire of items that it can make. Bowyer believes that the price "could drop to a few dollars as the number of self-replicating models increases exponentially." Other researchers at the University of California are working on a similar technology, called polymer mechatronics, and Intel Corp. has even devised clever shape-shifting blocks, called Dynamic Physical Rendering, which can fashion themselves into three-dimensional shapes.

What are the implications for manufacturing, transportation, commerce, and the global economy when people are able to print out a new set of dishes for a dinner party and then recycle those dishes into something different the next day? One consequence is that the software for building those products will become more valuable than the product itself. In essence, recipes (information) and not biscuits (physical objects) will be shipped around the world.

Another exciting ripple in the field of self-replication is occurring in robotics. Scientists at Cornell University are busily working away to develop a robot that can create a copy of itself. They have only developed a crude prototype, but the researchers envision that the principle of replication can be extended to create robots that could repair themselves in the event that they get damaged on bottom of the ocean or deep in space.

Even if self-replicating robots are a longer-term possibility, a more near-term possibility is biometmetic robots—robots that mimic the best of Mother Nature. Many of these advances were outlined in Chapter 8. Dr. Y. Bar-Cohen captures the potential perfectly: "In my vision for the field of robotics, I see one day when . . . biometmetric-legged robots can run as fast a cheetah, carry mass like a horse, climb cliffs like a gecko, reconfigure its body like an octopus, fly like a bird and dig tunnels like a gopher."

Yet another technological trend rippling on the edge of tomorrow is organic printing. Over time this could revolutionize the fields of agriculture and food production. Researchers at Utrecht University in the Netherlands are now growing artificial pork out of pig stem cells. The cost of a single pound of this pork is today quite high—between $1,000 and $10,000 a pound—but Jason Matheny, the director of New Harvest, a nonprofit that funds research on *in vitro* meat, believes the cost can someday be reduced to around a dollar.

As unappetizing or crazy as manmade pork might sound, it is possible that in the future people will prefer meat that is made in this manner. After all, because it does not require any antibiotics or fertilizer, it could be viewed as being more environmentally sustainable. And because it not would take the 10,000 pounds of feedstock it currently takes to grow a 1,000-pound pig, it might also be more affordable. As an added benefit, it is possible that the meat could be tailored for individual taste, and because no slaughtering would be involved in making the meat it would almost certainly be viewed as being more humane.

Exponential **INSIGHT**

As famed economist Joseph Schumpeter said, "Technology is not kind. It does not wait. It does not say please. It slams into existing systems and often destroys them . . . while creating a new system." From manufacturing and transportation to agriculture, education, and energy, many of today's largest industrial sectors are experiencing small ripples of change on their outer edges. Some of these ripples will move like a tsunami—which also starts small and gathers strength exponentially before slamming into its unsuspecting targets.

JUMP THE CURVE STRATEGY #48:
Jump out of the Water

To jump such a tsunami one must think big. When I speak here of thinking big, I am recalling the examples of Alexander Graham Bell who envisioned putting a phone in every home, Bill Gates and Paul Allen who dreamed of putting a personal computer—running Microsoft software—in every home, or even their present-day equivalents, people such as Nanosolar CEO Martin Roscheisen who wants to put a solar panel on every home, Jimmy Wales, the founder of Wikipedia, who wants to put a free online encyclopedia in everyone's home (in their own language), and Oh Sang-rok, the manager of South Korea's intelligent service robot project, who wants to put a robot in every home by 2010. But to think big, the exponential executive must be able on occasion to step into the next dimension.

Let me go a little further with the analogy of the carp swimming toward the ripple. Imagine for a moment that carp reached the ripple on the surface and for one brief, glorious moment broke free of the water and leapt into the air. The view would be astounding from the perspective of the carp. It would be the equivalent of seeing a new dimension. The sky, the sun, the moon, and the stars, not to mention the land and everything on it—insects, animals, and people—would offer vistas of an almost unbelievable and heretofore unimaginable new world.

So it is with the exponential economy. Yet, like jumping fish, a few remarkable people have been able to launch themselves into new worlds. Often their initial view is fuzzy, and the constraints of their existing knowledge limit their ability to articulate everything that is out there, but still they offer us a glimpse.

In 1945 Vannevar Bush, the science advisor to presidents Roosevelt and Truman, wrote a remarkable article entitled "As We May Think" for *Atlantic Monthly* outlining his view of a new world. In one prescient passage he wrote this: "Consider a future device for individual use, which is sort of a mechanized private file and library. It needs a name, and, to coin one at random 'memex' will do. A memex is a device in which an individual stores all his books, records, and communications, and which is mechanized so that it may be consulted with exceeding speed flexibility. It is an enlarged supplement to his memory."

It is now sixty-two years later, and the convergence of computer processing power, data storage, and wireless technology have now provided us the World Wide Web, which can be "consulted with exceeding speed and flexibility" to easily search much of the world's growing database of knowledge.

Now jump forward to November 2005. In an interview with the *Washington Post*, Larry Brin, half of the brain trust of Google, posed this question: "Why not improve the brain?" He went on to offer a partial answer as to how we might get there. "Perhaps in the future," he said, "we can attach a little version of Google that you just plug into your brain."

Crazy? Or is Brin thinking big? A teenager in St. Louis is already playing a video game controlled by thought alone. Consider also the advances that companies such as Cyberkinetics are making in the fields of neural implants and brain-machine interfaces and it is not much of a stretch to assume that such mind-control devices will soon be in demand not just by paraplegics or cyberpunks but by people looking for a realistic method to help keep pace with the growing amount of information and knowledge that is flooding onto the global grid every moment of every day.

Another scientist who was capable of thinking in a future dimension was the famed physicist Richard Feynman. In 1959 the Nobel Laureate gave a now-famous speech, entitled "There's Plenty of Room at the Bottom," in which he said, "The principles of physics, as far as I can see, do not speak against the possibility of maneuvering things atom by atom." He went on to note that his vision was only hampered "by our ability to see and manipulate things at the molecular and atomic level."

For almost two decades now those obstacles of being able to see and manipulate at the atomic level have slowly been eroding. Every day, scientists, researchers, and businesspeople all around the world are continuing to diligently toil away to bring Feynman's vision ever closer to reality.

In 1999 the U.S. government commissioned a group of this country's preeminent scientists to study nanotechnology and write a report about its possibilities. In the executive summary of their report they wrote: "Because of nanotechnology we will see computers a million times more powerful than those that exist today; a data storage device the size of a sugar cube capable of holding the entire contents of the Library of Congress; hundreds of cancer curing drugs; and materials 100 times strong than steel but one-sixth the density."

Since the report was published IBM and Hewlett-Packard have both demonstrated prototype devices of radically more powerful computers. Seagate has constructed a data storage hard drive about the size of a laptop computer that is capable of holding one-tenth of the Library of Congress. The first nano-based cancer drug is now on the market (with hundreds more working their way through the FDA pipeline). And the U.S. Army and others are exploring how to use carbon nanotubes—which are a hundred times stronger than steel—to construct everything from lightweight car frames and better-than-Kevlar bulletproof vests to cables that could theoretically hoist a space elevator into geosynchronous orbit.

A space elevator? Impossible, you say. Perhaps. Scientists have pointed out that carbon nanotubes have molecular flaws that might make such a device vulnerable to shredding, and still others have pointed out that the humans riding the space elevator would be exposed to troubling amounts of radiation on the long ride up. But perhaps the most serious obstacle is that to date the longest carbon nanotubes sheets that have been fashioned are only 30 meters in length. If, however, scientists can double the length of carbon nanotubes that can be grown every year for the next twenty-two years, such carbon nanotube cables could reach geosynchronous orbit by 2031.

Exponential **INSIGHT**

In 1979 Sir Arthur C. Clarke wrote a science fiction novel, *The Fountain of Paradise,* about a space elevator. When asked by a reporter at the time of publication about the possibility of such an elevator ever being constructed, his response was that "it will be built twenty-five years after everyone stops laughing." Well, Bradley Edwards, the CEO of Liftport, a private company dedicated to building the first space elevator, as well as some visionary officials at NASA have stopped laughing and are now devoting a considerable amount of time, money, and energy to achieve this vision. Interestingly the schedule calls for the space elevator to be operational in 2031—about right on schedule according to Clarke's prediction.

JUMP THE CURVE STRATEGY #49:
Forget the Pigeon

When Charles Darwin first proposed writing his landmark book on evolution, *The Origin of Species,* his editor suggested writing a book on pigeons because, in his words, "Everyone is interested in pigeons." Fortunately Darwin chose to ignore the advice. I am reminded of the story because even though Darwin's theory was proposing only that species make modest, incremental changes over long periods of time, it was—and in many circles still is—a revolutionary idea.

What then happens if evolution is not just incremental in nature but rather exponential? That, too, is a revolutionary idea—because it could impact us in our lifetimes.

We are now approaching a time when this exponential theory of evolution will be put to the test. If you accept the notion of evolution, you will agree that the earliest life appeared on earth approximately 4 billion years ago. Complex cellular organisms showed up 2 billion years ago, and the first multicellular organism about 1 billion years ago. The first reptiles and dinosaurs made their appearance 300 million years ago, the first primates 40 million years ago, homo sapiens 160,000 years ago, Cro-Magnon man 40,000 years ago, and civilization began about 10,000 years ago.

Thinking about this much progress over such an extended period of time is difficult. Years ago, Carl Sagan, the famed astronomer, offered up a "cosmic calendar" to make such progress more comprehensible to the layperson. He asked that they imagine the entire history of the universe being compressed into a single year.

Under this scenario the year would begin on January 1 with a bang—the Big Bang. Nothing much happens in our corner of the universe until about August when the sun makes it appearance. The earth itself does not show signs of any life until November when the first multicellular organisms begin wiggling about. Dinosaurs show up on Christmas Eve. At 10:15 A.M. on December 31, apes appear; humans begin walking upright at 9:24 P.M. Civilization appears at 11:59:20, writing is invented fifteen seconds later, Rome falls at 11:59:57, and the Renaissance happens one second before midnight. Everything else—the printing press, the steam engine, electricity, the computer, the Internet—is squeezed into the last second.

From this perspective, evolution can be seen as yet another exponential trend. So what does it mean? If you accept the premise that each additional doubling of an exponential trend contains as much change as all the previous changes, then it means that humans in our present form may not be the endpoint of humanity but merely a steppingstone to the next evolutionary stage.

If you are unwilling to accept that notion—and I understand any unease you might have—one must still concede that the accelerating rates of change in computers, biology, nanotechnology, and the cognitive sciences are converging in such a way that they hold the potential to usher in if not exponential change then a profound amount of progress.

LIVE LONG AND PROSPER

A few years ago, two researchers in the field of longevity were debating the idea that a child born in 2000 would live to 2150—or 150 years. One of the researchers, Steve Austad, argued that someone born at the start of the millennium would indeed live that long. His colleague took the opposite position. In an attempt to settle the debate, each man wagered $150. On the assumption that neither man would himself be around in 2150 to collect the winnings, they agreed to place the $300 in a bank account with the sum going to the winner's heirs in 2150.

It sounds like a frivolous exercise, but the answer of who will win the debate seems to me to be hidden in the prize. That is because after 150 years the $300 will grow to anywhere between $1.8 million and $485 million due to geometrical growth. (The lower figure assumes a 5 percent rate of return; the higher one uses the historical average annual rate of return for the stock market—10 percent.)

Now consider this: Even if medical information grows only 5 percent for the next century and a half, we will know roughly 6,000 times as much about human health in the year 2150 as we do today. Of course, medical knowledge is not growing at 5 percent, it is advancing closer to the 10 percent figure, which means society will possess even more knowledge. With this much new information is it possible that scientists and researchers will develop the understanding and the tools to keep someone alive to 150? Time will tell, but personally I wouldn't bet against it. Things that sound impossible today could very well become possible tomorrow.

Put another way, a great many bright people like Aubrey deGrey and other medical researchers aren't interested in pigeons. They are interested in contributing information that could push all of us up the next step in our evolutionary journey.

JUMP THE CURVE STRATEGY #50:
Embrace the Impossible

Up to this point in human history, man's time on this earth has been relatively scant—about eighty years, on average, for most of us. This small sliver of time hasn't allowed humans to observe evolution in any meaningful way. One habit that has emerged from this is that people tend to pay closer attention to short-term events while underestimating the importance of longer-lasting trends. Most people haven't worried about evolutionary change because it has occurred on such a slow scale as to be negligible.

For the reasons discussed throughout this book, this is about to change. The accelerating rate of technological change is nothing short of fantastic. One natural reaction to change is to resist it. Michael Mauboussin argues that this resistance to change allows people "to stop thinking about the issue—it gives [them] a mental break." He also argues that it allows people "to avoid the consequences of reason—namely, that they have to change."

But change we must. Change has been the overarching theme of this book for one simple reason: It is not simply the key to success; it is the key to survival.

CONCLUSION

Returning to Darwin for a moment, many people misinterpret the gist of his evolutionary message of the survival of the fittest. They think it means that the strongest and the smartest survive. This is not true. History clearly demonstrated that those who survive are not necessarily the strongest; rather, they are those who possess the ability to change and adapt to new conditions most quickly.

Years ago John Kenneth Galbraith wrote, "We associate truth with convenience . . . with what most closely accords with self-interest and personal well-being or promises to avoid awkward or unwelcome dislocations of life." He goes on to write that "economic behaviors are complex, and to comprehend their character is mentally tiring. Therefore, we adhere, as though to a raft, to those ideas which represent our understanding."

I close with these thoughts because the forces that are now shaping our economy are exponential in nature, like a hurricane that grows exponentially from the moment it is created until the time it smashes into people's homes. The exponential executive must discard certain ideas such as linear or incremental progress and embrace a future of exponential change or risk perishing.

Conclusion

To expect the unexpected shows a thoroughly modern intellect.

—Oscar Wilde

Richard Wurman, in his book *Information Anxiety,* wrote that a weekday edition of the *New York Times* contains more information than the average person was likely to come across in a lifetime in seventeenth-century England. Wurman wrote his book in 1989—the year the Berlin Wall came down. Thomas Friedman, in his book *The World Is Flat,* says that the falling of the Berlin Wall was just the first of ten forces that have since "flattened" the world. In a further bit of historical coincidence, in my first book on nanotechnology, *The Next Big Thing Is Really Small,* I cited November 9, 1989, (the day the Berlin Wall fell) as the official start of the nanotechnology era because it was on that day that two researchers at IBM first purposely manipulated atoms.

Looking back on the past eighteen years, few people would dispute that the amount of new information created and the methods for dispersing that knowledge have increased exponentially and heightened people's information anxiety. It is quite possible that now the amount of information in a daily *New York*

Times is equal to what someone in the eighteenth or nineteenth century consumed during their life.

Yet every day the advances continue to pick up steam. As proof let me take you through a short walk through the week of February 12–16, 2007—which happened to be the week I completed the original manuscript for this book.

The week kicked off with Intel Corp. announcing that it had built a single chip with eighty cores that was capable of completing 1 trillion computations every second. You might recall that it was just in 1996 that the company had proudly announced that an entire supercomputer had first achieved the milestone of one trillion calculations. The new chip will be available in 2008.

Not to be outdone, IBM announced on the same day that it had combined microprocessors and memory chips onto a single chip. In one fell swoop, the company effectively doubled microprocessor performance. The new chip is also expected to be on the market by 2008, where it will provide enhanced capability to gaming, networking, and multimedia applications.

On Tuesday, Novartis, the pharmaceutical giant, agreed to make available for free on the World Wide Web the 20,000 genes associated with diabetes that it had identified through the Human Genome Project. The company's rationale for doing so was simple; it figured that a lot more progress would be made in treating the disease by having the whole world interpret the data rather than keeping it secret. The power of the open-source ethos is now about to be unleashed on diabetes.

On Wednesday, Kaiser Permanente announced it was launching an ambitious multiyear study into the genetic and lifestyle factors that might give rise to a host of common diseases. It is the largest study of its kind, and it hopes to draw information from more than 500,000 individuals.

As this data is stored in a massive databases and run against complex algorithms, it is expected that much more will be learned about how people's genes interact with diet, exercise, and environmental factors to affect their health. The findings could be remarkable and are sure to take medical diagnosis and treatment to a new level.

In the field of the cognitive science, developments for this particular week were no less astonishing. Medical device giant Medtronic revealed that its engineers had developed an implantable "brain radio" to better monitor and control nervous disorders, and in Britain researchers announced they had discovered a new type of brain cell that can continuously regenerate. The development could lead to new treatments for Parkinson's, Alzheimers, and other brain-related diseases.

Meanwhile, over at Stanford University, Kwabena Boahen, a neuroengineer, unveiled an ambitious plan to create a silicon model of the cortex. Once constructed, this manmade brain will help scientists better understand how the human brain operates and how it does everything from performing complex computations and recognizing faces to understanding language.

It was only two decades ago that scientists first realized that transistors could be used to build circuits that mimicked the electrical properties of neurons, and in that short time we've learned 95 percent of everything we now know about the human brain. This week's advances and others like them will soon double that knowledge again.

On the manufacturing front, big things were happening in both Europe and Japan. Across the Atlantic, researchers announced two separate programs. The first was a project combining 3-D imagery with hand-tracking and speech recognition technology that could soon allow computer users to manipulate 3-D images in real time. If you recall the scene from the movie *Minority Report* (which was supposed to take place in 2054) in which Tom Cruise's character was moving around images and flipping files in a holographic form with just a flick of his wrist, you'll get the general idea of this technology.

Interestingly, in the movie Cruise was wearing haptic gloves, which just happened to be the second area of focus that European researchers were pursuing. The project, dubbed HAPTEX (HAPtic sensing of virtual TEXtiles) is working to create a glove that will allow the user to "virtually" feel different textiles. The technology, which was expected to be available in a prototype form by the end of 2007, could allow customers to browse in virtual stores such as those in Second Life and do everything from virtually lifting a couch and seeing it in a 3-D form to "feeling" the fabric.

On the other side of the world in Japan, Hitachi announced that it had created "powder" RFID tags. What is so interesting about these devices is that they are only .05 x .05 millimeters in size. If you are wondering how big a .05 millimeter tag is, it is smaller than the period at the end of this sentence or, as you might recall from the previous chapter, about the thickness of a piece of paper. The company expects to have working models on the market in 2008.

Of course, haptic and RFID technology, brain research, and computers will all continue to get exponentially better. Why am I so sure of this? Because on February 13, 2007, in Mountain View,

California, a small Canadian company, D-Wave, provided the first-ever demonstration of a quantum computer.

It was only a 16-qubit computer, but it was able to solve a Sudoku puzzle and, more impressively, it successfully searched for a large database for molecule that was similar to one used in the drug Prilosec. This suggests that quantum computers could be used to radically speed up the drug discovery process in the near future. It is also feasible that the quantum computer will be able to solve complex problems that are beyond the power of even tomorrow's most powerful conventional supercomputers.

D-Wave officials further noted that they believe quantum computing will follow a trajectory similar to Moore's law—which is to say that it will experience exponential growth. As proof, the company said it would have available a 32-qubit computer by the middle of 2007, a 512-qubit computer by early 2008, and a 1,024-qubit computer toward the end of 2008.

Among the many other things that such a quantum computer will be able to do is help design the next generation quantum computer. Believe me, the power that these quantum computers will possess is enough to make one's head spin. (I should note that because it is quantum in nature, if your head is spinning in a quantum world it will be spinning in opposite directions at the same time. Try wrapping your head around that!)

Recall now that all the aforementioned advances are the product of just a single week's worth of technological progress, and it reminds us that in order to effectively jump the curve the exponential executive will need to jump higher and farther on a continual basis. In fact, if D-Wave's advances in quantum computing continue to progress, in the not-too-distant future even jumping the curve won't be enough. The exponential executive will need to begin making *quantum leaps*, but such is the power and nature of exponential growth.

Jack Uldrich

P.S. To stay abreast of the latest exponential advances as well as learn about new methods of thinking, I encourage you to visit and bookmark the related Web site to this book: *www.jumpthe curve.net.*

Bibliography

GENERAL WORKS

Almond, Steve. *Candyfreak: A Journey Through the Chocolate Underbelly of America.* Harvest, PA: Harvest Books, 2005.

Anderson, Chris. *The Long Tail.* New York: Hyperion, 2006.

Bennis, Warren. *On Becoming a Leader.* Cambridge, MA: Perseus Books, 1989.

Benyus, Janine. *Biomimicry: Innovation Inspired by Nature.* New York: William Morrow, 1997.

Bryson, Bill. *A Short History of Nearly Everything.* London: Doubleday, 2003.

Capparell, Stephanie. *The Real Pepsi Challenge: The Inspirational Story of Breaking the Color Barrier in American Business.* New York: Free Press, 2007.

Christensen, Clayton. *The Innovator's Dilemma: When New Technologies Cause Great Companies to Fail.* Boston: Harvard Business School, 1997.

Christensen, Clayton, and Raynor, Michael. *The Innovator's Solution: Creating and Sustaining Growth.* Boston: Harvard Business School, 2003.

Coburn, Pip. *The Change Function: Why Some Technologies Take Off and Others Crash and Burn.* New York: Portfolio, 2006.

Collins, Jim. *Good to Great: Why Some Companies Makes the Leap—and Others Don't.* New York: HarpersCollins, 2001.

Diamond, Jared. *Guns, Germs, and Steel: The Fates of Human Societies,* New York: W. W. Norton & Company, 1997.

Dubner, Stephen, and Levitt, Steven. *Freakonomics: A Rogue Economist Explores the Hidden Side of Everything.* New York: William Morrow, 2005.

Enriquez, Juan. *As the Future Catches You: How Genomics & Other Forces Are Changing Your Life, Work, Health & Wealth.* New York: Crown Business, 2000.

Eppler, Mark. *The Wright Way: 7 Problem-Solving Principles from the Wright Brothers that Can Make Your Business Soar.* New York: AMACOM, 2004.

Feynman, Richard. *The Pleasure of Finding Things Out.* Cambridge, MA: Perseus Books, 1999.

———. *Surely You're Joking, Mr. Feynman.* New York: W.W. Norton & Company, 1985.

Friedman, Thomas. *The World Is Flat: A Brief History of the Twenty-First Century.* New York: Farrar, Straus and Giroux, 2005.

Gallivan, Brittany. *How to Fold Paper in Half Twelve Times: An 'Impossible' Challenge Solved and Explained.* Ponoma, CA: Historical Society of Ponoma Valley, 2001.

Garreau, Joel. *Radical Evolution: The Promise and Peril of Enhancing Our Minds, Our Bodies—and What It Means to Be Human.* New York: Doubleday, 2004.

Gelb, Michael. *Discover Your Genius: How to Think Like History's Ten Most Revolutionary Minds.* New York: Quill, 2003.

Gladwell, Malcolm. *The Tipping Point: How Little Things Can Make a Big Difference.* Boston: Little, Brown, and Company, 2000.

Gopnik, Alison, Patricia Kuhl, and Andrew Metzloff. *The Scientist in the Crib: What Early Learning Tells Us About the Mind.* New York: First Perennial, 2001.

Isaacson, Walter. *Benjamin Franklin: An American Life.* New York: Simon & Schuster, 2003.

Janis, Irving. *Groupthink: Psychological Studies of Policy Decisions.* New York: Houghton Mifflin Company, 1982.

Johnson, George. *A Shortcut Through Time: The Path to the Quantum Computer.* New York: Alfred A. Knopf, 2003.

Johnson, Steven. *Emergence: The Connected Lives of Ants, Brains, Cities, and Software.* New York: Scribner, 2001.

Kennedy, John, "Address at Rice University on Space Effort," September 12, 1962, *http://www.rice.edu/fondren/woodson/speech.html*

Kuhn, Thomas. *The Structure of Scientific Revolutions.* Chicago: The University of Chicago Press, 1962.

Kurzweil, Ray. *The Singularity Is Near: When Humans Transcend Biology.* New York: Viking, 2005.

————. *The Age of Spiritual Machines: When Computers Exceed Human Intelligence.* New York: Penguin Group, 1999.

Lewis, Michael. *Moneyball: The Art of Winning an Unfair Game.* New York: W.W. Norton, 2003.

Maslow, Abraham. *Toward a Psychology of Being,* third ed. New York: Wiley, 1998.

Mauboussin, Michael. *More Than You Know: Finding Financial Wisdom in Unconventional Places.* New York: Columbia University Press, 2006.

May, Ernest and Neustadt, Richard. *Thinking in Time: The Uses of History for Decision Makers.* New York: The Free Press, 1986.

Munger, Charlie, "A Lesson on Elementary, Worldly Wisdom as It Relates to Investment Management and Business." *Outstanding Investor Digest,* 1995.

Prahalad, C. K. *The Fortune at the Bottom of the Pyramid: Eradicating Poverty Through Profits.* Philadelphia: Wharton School Publishing, 2006.

Paulos, John Allen. *Innumeracy: Mathematical Illiteracy and Its Consequences.* New York: Farrar, Straus, and Giroux, 1988.

Rheingold, Howard. *Smart Mobs: The Next Social Revolution.* New York: Perseus, 2002.

Surowiecki, James. *The Wisdom of Crowds: Why the Many Are Smarter than the Few and How Collective Wisdom Shapes Business, Economies, Societies, and Nations.* New York: Doubleday, 2004.

Toffler, Alvin. *The Third Wave.* New York: Bantam Books, 1980.

Uldrich, Jack. *The Next Big Thing Is Really Small: How Nanotechnology Will Change the Future of Your Business.* New York: Crown Business, 2003.

———. *Into the Unknown: Leadership Lessons from Lewis and Clark's Daring Westward Expedition.* New York: AMACOM, 2004.

Waite, Stephen. *Quantum Investing.* New York: Texere, 2003.

Wurman, Richard. *Information Anxiety.* New York: Doubleday Publishing, 1989.

www.wearesmarter.org, Draft of online collabortive book, *We Are Smarter Than They.*

CHAPTER REFERENCES

Chapter 1

Colvin, Geoffrey. "Managing on the Edge." *Fortune* (October 2, 2006): 76.

McLaughlin, Laurianne. "Cores on a Chip." *Technology Review* (July/August 2006).

Huggins, James. "How Data is That?" *http://www.jamesshuggins.com/h/tek1/how_big.htm*

Greene, Kate. "Delivering DVDs in Seconds." *Technology Review* (June 19, 2006).

"Around the World in 800 Billion Bases." Wellcome Trust Sanger Institute Press Release. *http://www.sanger.ac.uk/Info/Press/2006/060117.shtml.*

"Winning Ways." *The Economist* (January 27, 2007): 80.

Chapter 2

Brown, David. "For First Woman with Bionic Arm, a New Life is Within Reach." *Washington Post* (September 14, 2006): A1.

"Scientists Complete Human Metabolome." UPI (January 24, 2007). *http://www.sciencedaily.com/upi/index.php?feed=Science&article=UPI-1-20070124-15033700-bc-canada-metabalome.xml*

Jackson, Daniel. "Dependable Software by Design." *www.scientificamerican.com* (May 22, 2006).

Markoff, John. "Brainy Robots Start Stepping into Daily Life." *New York Times*, (July 18, 2006).

Rosenberg, Scott. "Anything You Can Do, I Can Do Meta." *Technology Review* (January/February 2007): 36–44.

Chang, Alicia. "Online Astronomers Seek Out New Worlds." Associated Press, (January 16, 2007).

Koerner, Brendan. "Geeks in Toyland." *Wired.com* (January 4, 2006).

Deutschman, Alan. "Ears Wide Open." *Fast Company* (January 2007): 103–106.

Chapter 3

Tischler, Linda. "He Struck Gold on the Net (Really)." *Fast Company* (May 2002): 40.

LaMonica, Martin "IBM's Advance Team Does the Math." *CNET.com* (August 29, 2006).

"Distributed PC Computing Beyond SETI." *Technology Review. http://www .technologyreview.com/read_article.aspx?id=16960*

Berri, David. "The NBA's Secret Superstars." *New York Times* (June 10, 2006): A13.

St. John, Allen. "An NBA MBA." *Wall Street Journal.* (November 3, 2006).

"Scientists Use Math to Find Oil." *http://www.physorg.com/news74966906. html*

Norton, Quinn. "Software Helps Develop Hunches." *Wired News* (March 13, 2006).

McCue, Andy. "Marks & Spencer Extends RFID Tagging in Stores." *CNET News.com* (November 15, 2006).

Svensson, Peter. "Robot Parking Garage to Open in New York." Associated Press (January 30, 2007).

Gartner, John. "Nano Coatings Paint Green Future." *Wired.com* (February, 10, 2006).

McHugh, Josh. "How to Catch a Mavericks Wave." *Wired* (May 2006): 48–49.

Chapter 4

Marano, Hara. "The Power of Play." *Psychology Today* (July 1999).

Wolfe, Josh. "The Nanotech Insider." *Forbes* (June 4, 2004).

Salter, Chuck. "Just Add Inspiration." *Fast Company* (December/January 2007): 100.

Begley, Sharon. "Brainteasers May Help Researchers Determine What Spurs Creativity." *Wall Street Journal* (November 12, 2004).

Brand, Stewart. "Vinge's Singular Vision." *Technology Review* (July 31, 2006).

Schwartz, Evan. "Sparking the Fire of Invention." *Technology Review* (May 2004).

Christensen, Bill. "Smart or Scary? Software That Follows You." *LiveScience* (December 4, 2006).

Zaslow, Jeffrey. "What if Einstein Had Taken Ritalin? ADHD's Impact on Creativity." *The Wall Street Journal* (February 3, 2005).

Chapter 6

Terhune, Chad. "Pepsi, Vowing Diversity Isn't Just Image Polish." *Wall Street Journal* (April 19, 2005).

"Study Gives Us a New Perspective on the Powerful." *Science Daily* (January 11, 2007).

Nuland, Sherwin. "Do You Want to Live Forever?" *Technology Review* (February 2005): 37–45.

Morelle, Rebecca. "Scientists Divided Over Longeveity." *BBC News* (March 29, 2006).

Jaffe, Greg. "A Maverick's Plan to Revamp the Army is Taking Shape." *Wall Street Journal* (December 12, 2003): 1.

Chapter 7

Leonard, Abigail. "Meetings Make Us Dumber, Study Shows." *LiveScience* (February 22, 2007.)

Davis, Joshua. "Come to LeBow Country." *Wired* (February 2003).

Thompson, Clive. "Saving the World, One Video Game at a Time." *New York Times* (July 23, 2006).

"How Wrong Can You Be?" *Harvard Business Review* (April 2005): 118.

Rohwedder, Cecilie. "No.1 Retailer in Britain Uses 'Clubcard' to Thwart Wal-Mart." *Wall Street Journal* (June 6, 2006).

Sallek, Anna. "Doctors Use Google to Diagnose Disease: Study." *ABC News Online* (November 10, 2006).

Moore, Gary. "Exploring the Bottom of the Pyramid." *Perspectives in Business. http://www.stedwards.edu/business/pdf/Perspectives_V3N2_03.pdf*

"America the Creative." *The Economist* (December 23, 2006): 41.

Chapter 8

http://www.daimlerchrysler.com/Projects/c2c/channel/documents/783295_Gone_Fishin.pdf

Handwerk, Brian. "Artificial Silk Could be Used for Armor, More." *National Geographic News* (January 14, 2005).

Story, Derrick. "Swarm Intelligence: An Interview with Eric Bonabeau." *open2p2. com, http://www.openp2p.com/pub/a/p2p/2003/02/21/bonabeau.html*

Patel-Predd, Prachi. "Super Plastic Both Attracts and Repels Water." *Technology Review* (May 30, 2006).

Hambling, David. "Robotic Tentacles Get to Grips With Tricky Objects." *NewScientistTech* (May 8, 2006).

"Israel Developing Killer Bionic Hornet." Reuters (November 17, 2006).

Wilan, Ken. "Technology to Mimic Mother Nature." *Boston Globe* (August 22, 2005).

Chapter 9

Biello, David. "Back to the Future: How the Brain Sees the Future." *Scientific American* (January 2, 2007).

O'Connell, Vanessa. "The Gem War." *Wall Street Journal* (January 12, 2007).

Crossen, Cynthia. "Time Capsule May Give Insights into the Past—If Only it Can Be Found." *Wall Street Journal* (January 9, 2005).

Penenberg, Adam. "Technology: Boom, Bust and Beyond." *Fast Company* (March 2006): 105.

Booth, Robert. "Robo-builder Threatens the Brickie." *The Sunday Times* (January 14, 2007).

"The Economy's Good News: The Upside of Downsizing." *National Center for Policy Analysis* (February 25, 1998).

Waters, Richard "Why Nanotechnology is the Next Big Thing." *Financial Times* (March 29, 2005).

Chapter 10

Cassidy, John. "Mind Games." *The New Yorker* (September 18, 2006).

Clynes, Tom. "Dr. Nail Vs. The Monster." *Popular Science* (December 2006).

Sacks, Danille. "Leap of Faith." *Fast Company* (June 2006): 51–57.

Sandberg, Jared "Some Managers Make It Easy On Themselves With a Ready 'No'." *Wall Street Journal* (October 17, 2006): B1.

Chapter 11

Akst, Daniel, "Computers as Authors? Literary Luddites Unite!" *New York Times* (November 22, 2004).

Keats, Jonathon. "John Koza Has Built an Invention Machine." *Popular Science* (April 2006).

Ward, Mark. "Making Money From Virtually Nothing." *BBC News* (August 11, 2003).

Hopper, Simon. "The Machine That Can Copy Anything." *CNN.com* (June 2, 2005).

"Printable Robots: Advances In Inkjet Technology Forecast Robotic Technology." *Oh My News International* (June 21, 2006).

Joy, Bill. "The Dream of a Lifetime." *Technology Review* (August 2005).

Bailey, Ronald. "Forever Young." *Reason* (September 2002).

Index